Walking in the Spirit

FUCHSIA PICKETT, ThD, DD

CHARISMA
HOUSE

WALKING IN THE SPIRIT by Dr. Fuchsia T. Pickett
Published by Charisma House
Charisma Media/Charisma House Book Group
600 Rinehart Road
Lake Mary, Florida 32746
www.charismahouse.com

Cover design by Lisa Rae McClure
Design Director: Justin Evans

Library of Congress Control Number: 2015940473
International Standard Book Number: 978-1-62998-208-3
E-book ISBN: 978-1-62998-253-3

Portions of this book were previously published by Charisma House in *Presenting the Holy Spirit* by Dr. Fuchsia T. Pickett, copyright © 1997, ISBN: 978-0-88419-518-4.

15 16 17 18 19 — 9 8 7 6 5 4 3 2 1
Printed in the United States of America

Contents

Acknowledgments

I WOULD LIKE TO acknowledge:

The faithfulness of "my teacher," the Holy Spirit, who not only filled me with Himself, but also created within my spirit a desire to know Him personally and intimately, which thereby allowed Him to fulfill the mandate and mission in and through my life.

Carol Gwen Noe, of Blountville, Tennessee, a competent, Christlike teacher and minister of the Word and music, on whom the Holy Spirit laid the burden and commission to help me prepare for publication what she calls the "legacy of my life and ministry." Because of her faithfulness to Him and her unity of desire with me, this book has become a reality. Without her ministry in helping to prepare this book, it might never have been printed.

Rev. Sue Curran, pastor of Shekinah Ministries, Blountville, Tennessee, for constantly insisting that I not bury with me the revelation I have received and taught concerning the third Person of the Godhead, but that I write it as part of my legacy to the body of Christ. It is her persuasion that this "unique understanding of the person of the Holy Spirit" belongs to the body of Christ, and she has gently persisted in reminding me of my responsibility to leave it in good form for those who follow. I am grateful for her encouragement in this endeavor.

My beloved husband, Leroy*, for his support, love, and companionship that enables me to fulfill the purpose of God for my life. He is a constant encouragement as I preach, teach, dictate, and write, traveling with me throughout the nation and other countries.

Dr. Judson Cornwall*, my real spiritual brother and colleague, for editing the manuscript and for his words of encouragement and commendation to me.

---

* Leroy Pickett and Dr. Judson Cornwall passed away after Fuchsia Pickett wrote this book.

Foreword

I DOUBT IF I have ever met a person who spoke more of, depended more on, or enjoyed the Holy Spirit more than Dr. Fuchsia Pickett. The Spirit of God is not a theme to her; He is a Person of the Godhead who lives in her. She has studied His message, methods, and ministries with the keen eye of a research professor and with the emotions of a student deeply in love with the instructor.

Her inquiry has taken her beyond the common concepts of the gifts and fruit of the Spirit. What she offers us here of her life study on the Person and work of the Holy Spirit is a fresh insight on the infilling of the Spirit, and the subsequent outworking of that indwelling.

I am a contributor to this book, so I may speak with some bias, but I am convinced that much of what is written in this book is unknown by the great body of believers who have been baptized in the Holy Spirit in the past thirty years. Much emphasis has been placed on the unction of the Spirit, but little attention has been given to the function of God's Spirit.

Although this book contains some wonderful personal experiences, it is not a testimonial book. It is a theological treatise on the baptism of the Holy Spirit and how it should affect the daily life of believers. It is "must" reading for anyone serious about the ongoing work of the Spirit in his or her life and ministry.

—JUDSON CORNWALL*

---

* Judson Cornwall passed away after Fuchsia Pickett completed this book. He was a friend of hers for more than twenty years. He invited her to his church as a teaching evangelist on repeated occasions when he was a pastor in Oregon. Later he taught with her in her Bible school in Plano, Texas, and they repeatedly shared the platform as speakers in conferences and conventions. Cornwall claimed that she was "an anointed woman filled and thrilled with God's Word."

Introduction

OME READERS MIGHT think it rather abstract and impractical to write a book that answers the question, "Who is the Holy Spirit?" Others may deem it presumptuous of me to say, "I would like to present to you the Holy Spirit." To many people the Holy Spirit is nothing more than a name in a religious creed recited in liturgical services. To others He is merely a vague influence mentioned in the Scriptures. Even those Christians who think they know who the Holy Spirit is many times do not recognize Him as a divine Person. I do not blame anyone for thinking about the Holy Spirit in these ways, for I remember the time in my life when I too would have thought it strange to address the Holy Spirit as a personal friend and teacher. Even though I referred to Him as the third Person of the Godhead, when speaking theologically, He was not a real Person to me.

The doctrine of the Holy Spirit as a divine personality is not only extremely practical, but also fundamental to our knowledge of God and our relationship to Him. Anyone who knows God the Father and God the Son without having a true understanding of God the Holy Spirit has not attained the Christian conception of God, nor has he come to the fullness of Christian experience.

I must mention the doctrine of the Trinity here to give us a proper foundation for the study of the Holy Spirit. In Genesis 1:26 reference is made to the plurality that exists in the Godhead: "Then God said, "Let us make man in our image, after our likeness...." God referred to "Our" image and "Our" likeness, using plural pronouns to refer to Himself. Many such references confirm the reality of the Triune Godhead. Even the passage in Deuteronomy that some use to discount the validity of the Trinity, actually confirms the fact of the Trinity. We read there, "Jehovah our God is one Jehovah." (See Deuteronomy 6:4). The Hebrew word for God that is used here is a plural form. That indicates, in spite of the intense monotheism of the Hebrews, the plurality of persons in the one Godhead. So we refer to the Godhead in its original state, in the eons of eternity, as the triune Godhead. Our study here focuses on the Person of the Holy Spirit, but we cannot ignore His integral relationship to the triune Godhead.

The importance of understanding the Person of the Holy Spirit is seen first of all in His effect on our perspective of worship. If we think of the Holy Spirit as merely an impersonal influence or divine power, we will inevitably rob Him of the honor and the worship He is due. We will not relate to Him properly, or give Him the love and trust, and surrender and obedience, that we should. We need to acknowledge this third Person of the Godhead as He does His work on the earth, and yield to Him in complete obedience to His will.

Secondly, it is important that we not relate to the Holy Spirit only as an influence or power so we don't try to "use" Him, or "it," for our own purposes. This mistaken concept of the Holy Spirit inevitably leads to self-exaltation. It causes us to strut in pride, thinking that we have received the Holy Spirit and therefore belong to a superior order of Christians. Instead we need to think of Him correctly in the biblical way: as a divine Person of defined majesty and glory. Then we will relate to Him properly by asking such questions as, "How can I surrender more completely to the Holy Spirit?" and "How can the Holy Spirit possess me and use me in a greater way?" Relating to the Holy Spirit as a divine Person is one of the most fundamental truths of the Bible—one that we must understand if we are to enjoy right relationship with God. Many earnest Christians are going astray on this point. They are trying to get hold of some divine power that they can use according to their will or giftings instead of surrendering their lives to the Person of the Holy Spirit. True maturity in Christ only comes through cultivating a right relationship with the Holy Spirit.

We need to acknowledge the Holy Spirit as a divine Person of infinite majesty who has come to dwell in our hearts, take possession of us, and work out God's eternal plan and predestined will in us, for us, and through us, until we are a praise to the glory of the Father. Then we will experience true holiness in the reality of self-renunciation, self-abnegation, and self-humiliation. I know of no other truth that can humble us and put us on our faces before God more quickly than this: the blessed Holy Spirit is the third Person of the Godhead who has come to dwell in our hearts and to restore us to the image of our God as He, in His infinite wisdom, unfolds His predestined plan for our lives. Such love and infinite desire of the Godhead to dwell with mankind is incomprehensible to our finite minds.

Many Christians testify to the entire transformation of their lives and service to God when they become acquainted with the Holy Spirit as a Person. That is my personal testimony as well. After serving God as a Methodist professor and pastor for many years, I came into a fuller relationship with the Holy Spirit. I realized then that Someone had come to live in my life, Someone whom I was not personally or intimately acquainted with. When I surrendered my life completely to Him, He began to reveal to me that He had come to be my teacher. He had come to unveil the Christ who had been living

3

in me for seventeen years. It was then that I began to become intimately acquainted with the Holy Spirit as a Person.

People often misunderstand what we are saying when we refer to the Holy Spirit as a Person. They think we are saying that He has hands, eyes, and ears and operates in a physical body as we know it. But those physical characteristics are attributes of corporeality, not personality. The generally accepted attributes of personality are intellect, volition, and emotions; i.e., knowledge, will, and feelings. One who thinks, feels, and exercises his will is a person. We finite human beings will one day lose our corporeality. Our earthly life in this world will end, and we will depart from these bodies. That does not mean we will cease to be persons, however. The Bible says that when we are absent from the body, we are present with the Lord (2 Cor. 5:8). So we will be alive in the presence of the Lord without mortal bodies. The Scriptures ascribe to the Holy Spirit all the attributes of personality, which we have defined here, that make Him a divine Person. For example, knowledge is attributed to the Holy Spirit in the passage that says, "Likewise, no one knows the things of God, except the Spirit of God" (1 Cor. 2:11). The Holy Spirit is not just illumination or inspiration that comes to our minds so we can see truth. He is a Person who Himself knows the things of God and reveals them to us. We know also that the Holy Spirit came to instruct us, to become our teacher. Jesus said, " But the Counselor, the Holy Spirit, whom the Father will send in My name, will teach you everything and remind you of all that I told you" (John 14:26). It is our privilege today to have the Holy Spirit, a living Person, dwelling within us, opening the classroom of our spirits twenty-four hours a day and letting us ask about anything we want to know. He never closes the classroom and He never scolds us for asking. It is wonderful to know that, as we study the Bible, we have the divine Author of the Book to interpret it and to teach us its real and innermost meaning according to His divine knowledge.

Volition or will is attributed to the Holy Spirit in the Scriptures that teach us concerning the gifts of the Spirit: "But that one and very same Spirit works all these, dividing to each one individually as He will" (1 Cor. 12:11). The Holy Spirit came to earth to fulfill the will of God in the earth. Emotion is also attributed to Him in Paul's appeal to the Romans for prayer: " Now I ask you, brothers, through the Lord Jesus Christ and through the love of the Spirit, to strive together with me in your prayers to God on my behalf" (Rom. 15:30). Notice particularly the phrase, "the love of the Spirit." Isn't that a wonderful thought? It demonstrates that the Holy Spirit is not a blind influence or an "it." He is not tongues or gifts or just divine power. He is a divine Person, the third Person of the Godhead, living in us and loving us with the most tender love.

Have you ever thanked the Holy Spirit for His love? We think of God the Father who "so loved the world, that He gave His only begotten Son..." (John 3:16). We speak of Jesus's love for the church being so great that He suffered outside the city wall in order to sanctify unto Himself a glorious church. But have we considered "the love of the Spirit"? Often we thank our heavenly Father for His great love to us. We thank Jesus for loving us enough to die for us. Have we ever knelt in reverence to the Holy Spirit and thanked Him for His great love for us?

Yet we owe our salvation as truly to the love of the Spirit as we do to the love of the Father and the Son. If the Holy Spirit had not become the willing Servant to come to the world and seek out our lost condition and bring conviction to us, we could not have come to the Savior. I think we have missed a lot by not realizing who this blessed third Person of the Godhead is. We have not fully understood the love He has for us, and the hurt-love He still experiences as a servant bringing us back to the Father's house.

I think if I tried to briefly summarize the message of this book, I would shout to the church today: "This blessed Holy Spirit, the third Person of the Godhead, is not an 'it!' He is not a fleshly manifestation of 'religious' people jerking their bodies. He is not just tongues or gifts. He is much more than an 'influence.' He is the infinite, omnipotent, omniscient, omnipresent, eternal third Person of the triune Godhead! He is a divine Person!"

I'm sure this is not a new concept to many. But I wonder how it affects our lives in a practical way. Do we treat the Holy Spirit as a Person? Do we honor Him, love Him, and acknowledge Him? Have we learned to communicate with Him? Do we know communion with the Holy Spirit that the Bible teaches we can have? Do we think of Him as One who is alongside us, in us, helping us, comforting us? Have we experienced His divine comradeship? His companionship?

My whole purpose in writing this book is to present my friend and teacher as He has revealed Himself through the Scriptures to me personally. As we study the personality of this third Person of the Godhead as the Bible describes Him, it is my prayer that we come to know the blessed Holy Spirit in a more intimate and personal way and to learn to yield to Him and cooperate with Him more fully. It is with this desire that this book is presented to the body of Christ.

Chapter 1

When He Is Come

Divine Mission

. . . .

And when He is come, He will reprove the world
of sin, and of righteousness, and of judgment.

—JOHN 16:8, KJV

. . . .

JESUS DECLARED TO His disciples that it was expedient
that He go away. He promised them that if He went away,
He would send them a divine Comforter, the Holy Spirit
(John 16:7). Although they grieved at the thought of Jesus's
leaving, He continued to talk to them about the work of the
Holy Spirit who would come to comfort them. He told them
that the Holy Spirit would reprove the world of sin, of righteousness, and of judgment.

I wonder if it seemed strange to the disciples to relate
the idea of comfort and reproof so closely. The Greek word
for reprove can be translated also to mean convince, convict,
expose, and rebuke. Jesus taught that part of the Holy Spirit's
work is to reprove or convince men of sin, of righteousness,
and of judgment. Someone has wisely observed: "These three
things are the most difficult to impress on any man, for he can
always attempt to justify himself by asserting an inexcusable

motive for evil actions, or by pleading a relative scale of ethical standards in the place of absolute righteousness, thereby assuming that judgment is indefinitely deferred so that it is no real threat."[1] Such is the lost state of mankind for whom the Holy Spirit came to do His divine work. He must convict men of their lostness and blindness in these three areas of moral failure: sin, righteousness, and judgment.

"Of sin, because they do not believe in Me" (John 16:9). It is impossible for a person to produce conviction in the heart of another person. Only the Holy Spirit can reveal the deceitfulness of our hearts and make us realize the greatness of our iniquity in the eyes of a holy God. The particular sin to which Jesus is referring, the one of which the Holy Spirit will convict, is not what we have labeled "gross sins," those such as adultery, murder, stealing, or drunkenness. No, it is the sin of unbelief—that failure to believe in Christ as the Savior who alone can forgive us of our sins. Unbelief in Jesus Christ results in the rejection of God's only means of forgiveness and brings all the condemnation of other sins upon the one who fails to appropriate

Christ's salvation through faith. The sin of unbelief negates the efficacious, vicarious, substitutionary, mediatorial work of Calvary. This tragic fact makes unbelief the greatest sin.

As George Smeaton has so aptly stated it:

> The sin of unbelief is here described, with all the erroneous guilt attached to it, as a rejection of the proposal of reconciliation, as the chief and supreme sin, because a sin against the remedy, as sinful in itself, and as preventing the remission of all other sins…original and actual, with all their guilt, that are remissable through faith in Christ. But this sin involves the rejection of the graciously provided remedy; and final unbelief has

nothing to interpose between the sinner and righteous condemnation....The sin of unbelief is here described as if it were the only sin, because, according to the happy remark of Augustine, while it continues, all other sins are retained, and when it departs, all other sins are remitted.[2]

Only the convicting work of the Holy Spirit can bring us to a realization of our sinfulness, causing us to turn to Christ and cry for mercy. We can be thankful for His convicting power that turns us from darkness to light and convinces us that we need a Savior. That reality brings true comfort to a lost, sin-sick soul in its misery.

"Of righteousness, because I am going to My Father..." (John 16:10). The righteousness of which the Holy Spirit convinces mankind is not human righteousness, but Christ's righteousness. The resurrection and ascension of Christ into the presence of the Father attest to His righteousness. Had Jesus been an impostor, as the religious world insisted He was when they crucified Him, the Father would not have received Him. The fact that the Father did exalt Him to His right hand vindicated Him of the charges, the accusations, and railings the religious leaders and the multitude heaped upon Him when they crucified Him. It also proves that Jesus paid the full price for the sins of the whole world, which had been laid upon Him. Smeaton describes Jesus's sacrifice in this way:

> To convince the world of righteousness must mean that the Spirit gives convincing evidence, not merely that His cause was good, or that He is innocent, but that in Him is the righteousness that the world needs, the imputed righteousness that He graciously provided for us and becomes ours by faith?[3]

Jesus's return to the Father gave evidence that He had fully completed the task He had been sent into the world to do. He had provided righteousness for those who would believe on Him. Although we have to admit, with the prophet, that "our righteousnesses are as filthy rags" (Isa. 64:6, KJV), if we believe in Christ, He will justify us before the Father. Then we can live "just-as-if-I'd never sinned."

"*Of judgment, because the prince of this world is judged*" (John 16:11, KJV). Aren't you glad that verse reads "is judged"? It means the devil has already been judged and is now judged. Jesus said on another occasion, "Now is the judgment of this world: now shall the prince of this world be cast out" (John 12:31, KJV). Since Christ has judged the prince of this world, all who follow the devil will be judged as well. Because of that judgment, the world stands guilty of refusing to believe in Christ. Its condemnation is proclaimed by the righteousness that Christ exhibited in His going to the Father. Therefore, nothing but judgment awaits the world. The greatest demonstration of that judgment is that the prince of this world is judged.

The Holy Spirit has come, then, according to Jesus, to convict men of sin, of righteousness, and of judgment. Unfortunately even some Christians don't understand the nature of this reproving and convicting work of the Holy Spirit. The Holy Spirit does not function in the physical environment or atmosphere, apart from human vessels. He convicts men through the power of the written Word as it is read, and through the preached Word as it is heard. He does His convicting work, as well, through Spirit-filled believers who live godly lives as a testimony for righteousness before others who do not know Christ.

On the Day of Pentecost, when the disciples were filled

with the Holy Spirit, Peter stood up to preach to several thousand people who experienced the convicting power of the Holy Spirit through his message and so repented of their sins and were baptized. Because the Holy Spirit works through believers, it is imperative that each believer live a Spirit-filled life, walking in the Spirit. The Holy Spirit will be faithful to convict believers continually, as well, of the presence of sin in their lives and to help them cry out to be forgiven and delivered from its power.

PROGRESSIVE REVELATION OF GOD

We can hope to have insight concerning God only according to the ways God has chosen to reveal Himself to us. The Scriptures declare:

> God, who at sundry times and in divers manners spake in time past unto the fathers by the prophets, hath in these last days spoken unto us by His Son, whom He hath appointed heir of all things, by whom also He made the worlds.
> —HEBREWS 1:1–2

This passage teaches us that God's way of revealing Himself to mankind, after the time of the prophets, was through His Son, Jesus. Jesus Christ perfectly revealed God the Father. That same passage in Hebrews declares that Jesus is "the brightness of His glory, and the express image of Himself..." (Heb. 1:3). Jesus reinforced this truth when He said to His questioning disciples, "He who has seen Me has seen the Father" (John 14:9).

Do you see the progression here in the revelation of God to man? The Father is revealed to us by the Son, and the Son is revealed to us by the Holy Spirit. G. Campbell Morgan states this truth in an interesting way; he refers to Jesus as the revelation of the Father and calls the Holy Spirit the "interpretation of the revelation."[4] Although the Godhead is one Triune God, each member has His particular place and function regarding redemption as revealed in the Scriptures. Jesus said of the Holy Spirit:

> But when the Spirit of truth comes, He will guide you into all truth. For He will not speak on His own authority. But He will speak whatever He hears, and He will tell you things that are to come. He will glorify Me, for He will receive from Me and will declare it to you. All that the Father has is Mine. Therefore I said that He will take what is Mine and will declare it to you.
> —JOHN 16:13–15

According to this passage, the Holy Spirit did not come to minister only to the sin question. Jesus continued to declare to His disciples the work of the Holy Spirit, describing Him as the Spirit of truth. Note the five things that Jesus said the Holy Spirit would do: (a) He will guide you into all truth; (b) He will not speak on His own initiative (meaning out of His own resources), but whatever He hears, He will speak; (c) He will show to you what is yet to come; (d) He shall glorify Jesus, for He shall take of Jesus's; and (e) shall show it to you. These are emphatic statements concerning what the Holy Spirit will do—not maybe so, not might or perhaps—but that He will do. When the Holy Spirit comes to our individual hearts and to our churches, we can expect Him to work in these wonderful ways to reveal Jesus to us.

The Work of the
Holy Spirit in Christ

Before we relate the coming of the Holy Spirit to our own lives, it will be profitable for us to understand the integral relationship of the Holy Spirit to the Person and ministry of our Lord Jesus. This relationship is especially significant as it pertains to the humanity of Jesus. The Holy Spirit has little to do with the deity of our Lord, for Jesus was God Himself. As John so clearly declares, "In the beginning was the Word, and the Word was with God, and the Word was God" (John 1:1). But the Holy Spirit does have much to do with Christ's human nature as Christ humbled Himself to take upon Him the form of a servant in order to bring the plan of redemption to mankind (Phil. 2:7–8).

In His birth

Of course, we understand that Christ did not have His beginning in the manger in Bethlehem. He existed from all eternity and before eternity, back in the eons of the ages before time began. He who always existed was sent by the Spirit into the world (Isa. 48:16). It was the Holy Spirit who facilitated His coming, for Jesus was conceived by the Holy Spirit. When the angel of the Lord appeared to Mary, he declared: "The Holy Spirit will come upon you, and the power of the Highest will overshadow you. Therefore the Holy One who will be born will be called the Son of God" (Luke 1:35). Then the angel of the Lord appeared to Joseph, her husband-to-be, saying, "Joseph, son of David, do not be afraid to take Mary as your wife, for He who is conceived in her is of the Holy Spirit" (Matt. 1:20).

The divine conception of the Lord Jesus did not involve

calling a new being into life as when other human beings are born. This divine One who had existed eternally, through His conception, was now entering into relationship with mankind as a human being with human nature. He was not conceived in sin, for His conception was holy, wrought by the Holy Spirit. Paul explains clearly that Christ, who was as God and equal with Him, emptied Himself and "took upon Him the form of a servant, and was made in the likeness of men" (Phil. 2:7, KJV).

This Greek word for emptied means "parked" or "set aside." Christ's conception involved His willingly laying aside His deity and taking on a human nature. He set aside His deity when He became man, completely yielding Himself to the Holy Spirit and being empowered by Him. Jesus was fully God and fully Man, but He lived by the power of the Holy Spirit while on the earth, having emptied Himself of His divine powers. Although He was still Christ, the Creator of the universe, He lived on the earth as Jesus, the Man, empowered by the Holy Spirit. He said of Himself, " I can do nothing of Myself" (John 5:30). It is important that Christians understand this reality, that we not look at Jesus's victorious life and say, "Yes, but He was God." In living His life as a man, Jesus taught us that the source of victory is being filled with, empowered by, and obedient to the Holy Spirit at every moment.

Without the Holy Spirit, even the incarnation of Jesus through conception would not have been possible. Likewise in our regeneration, our new birth is impossible without the Holy Spirit creating the life of God in us.

His presentation at the temple

Mary and Joseph took Jesus to Jerusalem to present Him at the temple, fulfilling the law by offering the sacrifice required for a firstborn male (Luke 2:23). There was an old priest there named Simeon who had served God devoutly. He prayed that he not die until he see the salvation of God. "It was revealed to him by the Holy Spirit that he would not die before he had seen the Lord's Christ" (v. 26). The Scriptures say that Simeon went into the temple "by the Spirit" (v. 27) on the day that Mary and Joseph took Jesus to present Him according to the law.

The Holy Spirit revealed to Simeon that this baby was indeed the Christ for whom he had been waiting. This godly priest began to prophesy over Jesus, to the amazement of His parents. Then Simeon declared that he was ready to die, for he had seen the salvation of God. The Holy Spirit also included Anna, the prophetess, in this revelation of Jesus's coming. She had served God night and day with fastings and prayers, and He revealed to her that this babe was the long-awaited Savior. She began to give thanks to God and to tell everyone who was looking for redemption that Jesus, the Christ, had indeed come (vv. 36–38). Perhaps the revelation of Jesus to these two is more striking because of its contrast to all those who did not recognize His coming. Only those who knew God by the Spirit enjoyed this initial revelation.

His growth to maturity

Jesus was not created as an adult like the first Adam was. He grew and developed as any other child grows, except that He did not possess any of the detriments of a sinful nature. Luke tells us, "And the Child grew and became strong in spirit, filled with wisdom. And the grace of God was upon Him" (v. 40). Jesus grew into a beautiful young man filled with such wisdom that He astonished the temple rabbis of Jerusalem when He was only twelve years old. He was hearing them and asking them questions, and "all who heard Him were astonished at His understanding and His answers" (v. 47). Jesus's understanding of the Scriptures was not just a result of childhood studies common to Jewish boys, but was the result of the work of the Holy Spirit in Him. Isaiah's prophecy hundreds of years earlier was beginning to be fulfilled when the boy Jesus was in the temple that day, though it would be realized in its fullest sense after His baptism. Isaiah prophesied:

> And there shall come forth a shoot from the stump of Jesse, and a Branch shall grow out of his roots. The Spirit of the LORD shall rest upon him, the Spirit of wisdom and understanding, the Spirit of counsel and might, the Spirit of knowledge and of the fear of the LORD....
> —ISAIAH 11:1–3

Christ's divinity could not grow or develop in any way; it was perfect and complete. But His humanity did develop and increase in its abilities by the power of the Holy Spirit.

His baptism

John the Baptist was baptizing people in the Jordan when he looked up and saw Jesus coming to him to be baptized. Although John did not feel worthy to baptize the Lamb of God, Jesus said to him, "Let it be so now, for it is fitting for us to fulfill all righteousness" (Matt. 3:15). When John baptized Jesus, the Spirit of God descended like a dove and lighted upon Him. A voice from heaven confirmed that Jesus was His beloved Son in whom He was well pleased (Matt. 3:16–17). The Holy Spirit was equipping Jesus, in His baptism, for His earthly ministry that was to follow. But first He led Him into the wilderness to be tempted by the devil.

His temptation

The Scriptures clearly indicate that the Holy Spirit not only led Christ into the wilderness (Matt. 4:1), but that all the time Christ was there the Holy Spirit was with Him, enabling Him to overcome the severe temptations of the evil one. Luke tells us that Jesus was full of the Holy Ghost when He was led by the Spirit into the wilderness (Luke 4:1). By the power of the Holy Spirit, Jesus's human nature was given the strength to withstand the enemy and to overcome the severe temptations placed before Him. His victory was not because of qualities of His divine nature infused into His human nature, for then He would no longer have been a man. Being a complete man, He relied only on the indwelling Holy Spirit for His ability to resist the temptations of the evil one. When He had conquered temptations of the devil by declaring, "It is written," Luke tells us He "returned in the power of the Spirit to Galilee" (v. 14).

We know that Jesus was not cornered by the devil. He was led out, or as Mark said, driven by the Spirit into the wilderness to meet the enemy (Mark 1:12). This can be very instructive for believers who find themselves in a place of testing or temptation. The Christian who is subject to temptation or personal testing is not necessarily out of the will of God. There are times in life that we must face the tempter, as Jesus did, with a clear response: "It is written." As we allow ourselves to be filled with the Holy Spirit, we have the same possibility of victory as Jesus, who conquered the devil through the power of the Holy Spirit.

His ministry

The Holy Spirit anointed Jesus with power for His earthly ministry as well. Jesus, Himself, attributed His works to the divine anointing of the Holy Spirit who worked through Him when He stood in the temple and declared:

> The Spirit of the Lord is upon Me, because He has anointed Me to preach the gospel to the poor; He has sent Me to heal the broken-hearted, to preach deliverance to the captives and recovery of sight to the blind, to set at liberty those who are oppressed; to preach the acceptable year of the Lord.
> —LUKE 4:18–19

Peter also preached this truth to the house of Cornelius, telling them that "God anointed Jesus of Nazareth with the Holy Spirit and with power, who went about doing good and healing all who were oppressed by the devil, for God was with Him" (Acts 10:38). It was through the divine power of the Holy Spirit that Jesus could do miracles. The Pharisees had accused Jesus of casting out demons by the power of Beelzebub, the prince of demons. But Jesus showed them the foolishness of thinking that Satan would cast out himself. Then He instructed them that if He "But if I cast out demons by the Spirit of God, then the kingdom of God has come upon you" (Matt. 12:28). His ministry was performed by the power of the Holy Spirit who is also resident within us today as Spirit-filled believers.

His transfiguration

> Jesus took Peter, James, and John his brother and brought them up to a high mountain alone, and was transfigured before them. His face shone as the sun, and His garments became white as the light.
> —MATTHEW 17:1–2

When Jesus was transfigured before His disciples, the unveiling of the glory of God that was in Him was seen in His human vessel. That unveiling was done by the blessed Holy Spirit. How awesome that the manifested presence of the glory of the infinite God was seen for a few moments by the disciples! Is it any wonder that Peter wanted to build three tabernacles?

His death

It was not enough that Jesus suffer and die for our sins; He had to do so in the proper manner. Abraham Kuyper expresses this fact so clearly:

> Christ did not redeem us by His suffering alone, being spit upon, scourged, crowned with thorns, crucified, slain. This passion was made effectual to our redemption by His love and voluntary obedience. Hence there was in Christ's suffering much more than mere passive penal satisfaction. Nobody compelled Christ. He who partook of the divine nature could not be compelled but offered Himself voluntarily. "Lo I come to do thy will, Oh God, in the volume of the Book it is written of Me."[5]

Jesus was empowered and enabled by the Holy Spirit to offer this acceptable sacrifice for the sins of the whole world. The Scriptures, comparing Jesus's sacrifice to that of the blood of bulls and goats, declare: "How much more shall the blood of Christ, who through the eternal Spirit offered Himself without blemish to God, cleanse your conscience from dead works to serve the living God" (Heb. 9:14). The perfection of Christ's sacrifice in His obedient, loving attitude was made possible by the eternal Spirit of God. Without the enabling of the Holy

Spirit, the Man, Jesus, could not have offered Himself as a perfect sacrifice to God.

His resurrection

Sometimes the resurrection of Jesus is attributed to the Father (Acts 2:24). Other times it is said to be the work of the Son Himself (John 10:17–18). But the resurrection is also in a special way the work of the Holy Spirit. Our intent is not to separate the Godhead in our thinking, but to show the interrelatedness of Their working together to accomplish the redemption of mankind. Paul writes, "But if the Spirit of Him who raised Jesus from the dead lives in you, He who raised Christ from the dead will also give life to your mortal bodies through His Spirit that lives in you" (Rom. 8:11). The Spirit of God working with the Father gave resurrection life to Jesus. He still offers that same resurrection life to every believer who will receive from His hand the things of Jesus.

Birthing the Church

Jesus stated clearly that if a man is not born of water and of the Spirit, he cannot see the kingdom of God (John 3:5). Natural life is given by natural birth. Spiritual life can only be given by being born again from above by the Spirit of God.

Adam lost his spiritual life when he sinned. Many believe it was the indwelling presence of the Holy Spirit that he lost. God had warned that death would follow disobedience to His word. Because of his sin Adam was left in spiritual darkness and was spiritually dead. Myer Pearlman describes the terrible results of this loss of the Holy Spirit in unregenerate man since the fall:

In relation to understanding, the unconverted cannot know the things of the Spirit of God (1 Cor. 2:14). In relation to the will, he cannot be subject to the law of God (Rom. 8:7). In relation to worship, he cannot call Jesus Lord (1 Cor. 12:3). As regards practice, he cannot please God (Rom. 8:8). In regard to character he cannot bear spiritual fruit (John 15:4). In regard to faith he cannot receive the spirit of truth (John 14:17). This new spiritual life is imparted to the believer through the indwelling Holy Spirit which is the mark of a New Testament Christian. "But ye are not in the flesh but in the Spirit if so be the Spirit of God dwelleth in you..." (Rom. 8:9). One of the most comprehensive definitions of a Christian is that he is a man in whom the Holy Spirit dwells. His body is the temple of the Holy Ghost in virtue of which experience he is sanctified as the tabernacle was consecrated by Jehovah's indwelling (1 Cor. 6:19). This is not to be confused with the baptism of the Holy Spirit which is an outpouring of the Spirit *after* salvation. It is not the impartation of spiritual life but rather power for spiritual service.[6]

Jesus's death and resurrection made it possible for all the effects of the fall of man to be reversed. We have only to believe on Him and be born again from above by the Spirit of God to begin living a life that God ordained for us from the beginning. Today His church on the earth is intended to be the body of Christ demonstrating to the world the supernatural life that is received through the Holy Spirit.

Commissioning the disciples

During the forty days He remained on earth after His resurrection, Christ also gave commandments to His disciples by the power of the Holy Spirit. Luke declares, "Until the day in which He was taken up, after that He through the Holy Ghost had given commandments unto the apostles whom He had chosen" (Acts 1:2, KJV). It was "through the Holy Ghost" that the Lord Jesus gave the commandments to the disciples, commissioning them and sending them forth. This teaches us how vital the power of the Holy Ghost is today to the ministry of the servants of the Lord.

As the Holy Spirit guides each Christian who is serving God, it is wonderful to realize that it is the voice of Jesus speaking to them as He did when He commissioned His first disciples. It is the same Jesus who commanded those first disciples who is today guiding, commanding, commissioning, and directing His servants by the same blessed Holy Spirit. We are not dependent upon the physical presence of the Lord to be led by Him. Our guidance comes, as it did then, by the work of the Holy Spirit in our lives.

Baptizing the Church

Perhaps the most important thing that Jesus has done for His followers, after having purchased their redemption by His death and resurrection, is to baptize them with the Holy Spirit. John the Baptist declared to his followers that when the Lamb of God comes, "He will baptize you with the Holy Spirit and with fire" (Matt. 3:11). As necessary as the Holy Spirit's presence was in all the ministry of our Savior, it is no wonder He was so intent that those who carry on His work would also be empowered by the same mighty Holy Spirit.

It is indeed wonderful that believers today have this same Spirit, this same empowering, and this same anointing. How else could His work be accomplished? Jesus said, "He who believes in Me will do the works that I do also. And he will do greater works than these, because I am going to My Father" (John 14:12). He made provision for believers to be empowered by the Holy Spirit in the same way He was, and to do greater works than He did. I personally cannot do a greater miracle than Jesus. By "greater works" is meant that through many people, the church, more miracles will be accomplished. The corporate body of Christ can minister to multitudes that Jesus, as one Man, could not reach. As the head of His body, the church, Jesus knew that greater works would be accomplished through God's eternal plan for a glorious church on earth when He returned to His Father.

Progressive sanctification

The Holy Spirit's work is to first bring light to the darkness of unbelievers, lovingly wooing them to accept the sacrifice of Jesus. He also bears witness to the believer who has been born again and is now a child of God. All this takes place in regard to our salvation when we are born again. Then, subsequent to regeneration, the Holy Spirit begins to do a specific work that is different from that of the new birth. He begins to sanctify the believer, making him holy in thought, motive, and deed. This is a beautiful process that takes place as He changes us "from glory to glory" and imparts to us the character of our Lord Jesus Christ, bringing us to maturity. In order to accomplish this work, the Holy Spirit enables us to mortify the deeds of the flesh.

The Scriptures teach clearly that if we live after the flesh we will die, but if we through the Spirit do mortify the deeds of the body, we shall live (Rom. 8:5–13). The word *carnal* in the Scriptures describes that which is fleshly, pertaining to the old man, our Adamic nature. That is the nature the Christian must endure until the Holy Spirit comes to enable him to

23

mortify his flesh and live victoriously in the Spirit. The Holy Spirit's work is to restore us into the image of God, producing His character in us as we continually yield ourselves to Him.

THREEFOLD REVELATION

The Holy Spirit has come to reveal the life of our precious Lord Jesus (a) to us, (b) in us, and (c) through us. As He does this precious threefold work, Christ will be able to live His life in us and through us. In the first aspect of this threefold revelation of Jesus Christ, the Holy Spirit reveals Jesus to the believer, which results in regeneration, as we have discussed. Then He comes to produce the fruit of the Spirit in the believer so that the life of our Lord Jesus becomes our life. The fruit of the Spirit is a description of the character of Christ (Gal. 5:22–23). In order to produce the character of Christ in us, He enables us to exchange our self-life for the Christ-life, thereby sanctifying us. As this fruit abounds in the life of the believer, he is growing unto the measure of the stature of the fullness of Christ (Eph. 4:13).

Then the Holy Spirit works through believers in the ministry of service to the body of Christ and to the world. Through His baptism, He equips us to minister to others by giving us revelation of the Word of God and by helping us to pray according to the will of God. He gives spiritual gifts for this purpose and anoints us for the fulfilling of His purposes. We must remember, however, that the Holy Spirit never magnifies Himself or any human vessel through whom He operates. He came to magnify and glorify, extol and honor the Person and ministry of our Lord Jesus Christ. Whenever the Holy Spirit is truly having His way, Christ alone is exalted.

On the Day of Pentecost Peter declared, "Therefore, let

all the house of Israel assuredly know that God has made this Jesus, whom you have crucified, both Lord and Christ" (Acts 2:36). Jesus has been exalted to the right hand of the Father, and the Holy Spirit has come to magnify Him. In Old Testament times God was magnified through the law and the prophets. Then when Jesus came in the flesh, He was the manifestation of God to the world. Now God manifests Himself to the world through the Holy Spirit's revelation of Christ through human vessels, believers who allow the character of Christ to be developed in their lives.

When He is come! What a precious reality awaits every heart and church that gives the Holy Spirit His rightful place. There is no other way to know God except the Spirit of God reveal Him to our hearts. As we prepare to seek Him, we can be assured that He will come, for it is His will to reveal Jesus to every seeking heart. The Holy Spirit calls every person to come to God and receive full redemption as Christ provided it. Our positive response to Him will assure us of a divine relationship with God that He intended for us to enjoy.

Chapter 2

The Baptism of the Holy Spirit

Divine Enduement With Power

. . . .

For John baptized with water, but you shall be baptized
with the Holy Spirit not many days from now.

—ACTS 1:5

. . . .

THE WORD "BAPTISM" comes from the Greek word *baptizo*, which means "to be put into or buried into, made a participant or partaker." It does not mean being poured upon, as some have interpreted it to mean. Baptism involves three distinct elements. First there is a baptizer; second, a candidate; and third, an element into which the candidate is baptized. Baptism cannot occur with only one person present; there must be a candidate and a baptizer. Several different baptisms are taught in the Scriptures where these three elements are present to effect true baptism.

DOCTRINE OF BAPTISMS

The Scriptures refer to the doctrine of baptisms in the plural form of the word. They teach us that baptisms are among the foundation stones of our faith. For example, we are admonished to leave the doctrine of baptisms and other foundational teachings to go on to maturity (Heb. 6:1–2). It follows, then, that if we are not settled in these basic doctrines, we cannot mature properly. Is a person's spiritual foundation solid, who has not been a participant in all the baptisms? No. To become mature Christians, we must first embrace these foundational doctrines. God intends for our lives to become strong "spiritual buildings" for the purpose of Christ inhabiting them.

If a foundation stone is missing, or if it does not fit properly, that building will be shaky. There is nothing wrong with going to God and saying, "My foundation is not secure. If I need a stone changed or put in, please do it. I don't want to be shaken when the winds come." In times of testing the house that is not secure on its foundation will fall.

If the foundation stone of repentance is not laid correctly in our lives, for example, we won't be stable in our walk with God. Without the assurance that we are born again and at peace with God, we will realize one day that we have been trying to live a lifestyle we don't have the power to live. Nothing can substitute for repentance as the basis for peace with God. How are we going to *walk* in the Spirit, be *led* by the Spirit, *abide* in the Spirit, and *cooperate* with the Spirit if we are not first born again?

Some have never identified themselves with Christ's death by participating in water baptism. That foundation stone is lacking in their lives. Others need to be endued with power from on high—baptized in the Holy Spirit. And all must take up their cross daily and follow Christ even into the baptism of suffering, yielding to the Holy Spirit in their trials and learning to exchange their lives for Christ's. Only as these foundation stones are properly laid can believers expect to mature in Christ.

As we observe briefly these biblical baptisms, we are not discussing them in order as we experience them. For example, some people receive the baptism in the Holy Spirit before participating in water baptism; others receive water baptism first. The Scriptures cite instances of these baptisms happening in both orders.[1] Yet each of these baptisms needs to be a part of our personal experience if we expect to fulfill God's purposes for our lives.

Baptism of repentance

Jesus referred to the baptism that John preached as the *baptism of repentance*.[2] There were believers in the New Testament who were asked with what baptism they were baptized, and they replied, "with the baptism of John" (see Acts 18:25). John the Baptist came to "prepare the way of the Lord; make His paths straight" (Matt. 3:3). Closer study shows that he preached a fivefold message. First, he preached *repentance*, crying out, "Repent, for the kingdom of heaven is at hand" (v. 2). Second, he preached *remission of sins*, baptizing those in water who confessed their sins (v. 6). Third, he preached restitution for wrongdoing (Luke 3:11–14); and fourth, he preached the *receiving of the Holy Spirit* when Jesus came. John the Baptist declared, "I indeed baptize you with water. But One mightier than I is coming, the strings of whose shoes I am not worthy to untie. He will baptize you with the Holy Spirit and with fire" (v. 16). Fifth, he preached *righteousness*, crying, "'Make straight the way of the Lord,' just as the prophet Isaiah said" (John 1:23). The baptism of John is the first baptism every person must experience to become a born-again Christian. Repentance is the requirement for coming to Jesus.

The Scriptures teach that through repentance, not only are we born again, but we also are baptized into the body of Christ, the family of God. The apostle Paul wrote to the Corinthians, "For by one Spirit are we all baptized into one body..." (1 Cor. 12:13). What does that mean? Being placed into the family of God is a real happening. It places us into the church, a living organism of which Christ is the head. The Word, the seed of God, is placed into our dead spirits and we are quickened and made alive, born of His Spirit. In that supernatural quickening, we become a part of His body, baptized into the body of Christ.

We can easily define the three elements of baptism in this experience. The Holy Spirit is the baptizer, and we are the candidates for baptism. What is the element into which the Holy Spirit baptizes us? The body of Christ, the church. We are dependent upon the work of the Holy Spirit for the very initiation of our life in God as well as for every aspect of its development. Thank God for this convicting power of the Holy Spirit that shows us our sin and cleanses us when we confess it. Through the gift of repentance, the Holy Spirit is able to baptize us into the body of Christ.

Baptism in water

The second baptism we see in the Scriptures is *baptism in water*. This baptism follows our baptism into the body of Christ; it is a public demonstration that we are following Jesus's example in baptism.[3] In water baptism, of course, the baptizer is the minister, the candidate is the believer, and water is the element into which we are baptized. Although these three elements all pertain to the natural realm as opposed to the spiritual, we must not think that this baptism is merely a physical ceremony.

Water baptism is a spiritual reality. It is an experience of our being identified with Christ. It is our testimony of declaring that our old man is identified with Christ in His death, burial, and resurrection. We miss the significance of our identification with Christ if we believe that water baptism is only an external ceremony. Our participation in water baptism makes us a partaker of this identification with Christ in His death.

God doesn't ever ask us to play-act. Because water baptism is a spiritual experience, when we are baptized in water we should expect a change to take place in our lives that will declare to the world that salvation is working in us. It is a time of appropriating the greater aspect of the redemptive work of Christ: an identification with the death of our self-nature. In this act we declare that our natural self-life is dead, and we become a partaker of His death for our death. The circumcision of our hearts begins with this obedience to follow Christ in water baptism. God begins cutting away the sinful and destructive self-life as we raise a tombstone in that watery grave and declare, with John, "He must increase, but I must decrease" (John 3:30).

Baptism into the Holy Spirit

Third, there is the *baptism into the Holy Spirit*, which we want to study in more depth in this chapter. To properly define this baptism, we must address the erroneous teaching of some who believe that baptism into the Holy Spirit is the same as our baptism into the body of Christ. Understanding the three elements involved in baptism helps to clarify this confusion.

Of course, the candidates who are believers in Christ are the same for both the baptism into the body of Christ and the baptism of the Holy Spirit. It is the baptizer who is different. As we have seen, the Holy Spirit baptized us into the body of

Christ. According to the Scriptures, however, it is Jesus who baptizes us into the Holy Spirit. John declared, "I indeed baptize you with water. But One mightier than I is coming, the strings of whose shoes I am not worthy to untie. He will baptize you with the Holy Spirit and with fire" (Luke 3:16). In this baptism the Holy Spirit becomes the divine element into whom we are baptized. After the Holy Spirit baptizes us into the body of Christ, it is Christ who baptizes us into the Holy Spirit, filling us to overflowing with the third Person of the Godhead.

So we see the three members of the Godhead working in the redemption of a soul. Jesus taught, "If a man loves Me, he will keep My word. My Father will love him, and We will come to him, and make Our home with him" (John 14:23). He also said that the Holy Spirit "lives with you, and will be in you" (v. 17). The Father, the Son, and the Holy Spirit, the entire Godhead, dwell in the believer. They are in us and we are in Them—part of the family of God.

Baptism of suffering

A final baptism that we must mention as taught in the Scriptures is the *baptism of suffering.* Jesus said, "But I have a baptism to undergo, and how distressed I am until it is accomplished!" (Luke 12:50, NAS). He was, of course, referring to His death on the cross. Jesus knew He would have to endure a baptism of suffering because that was the purpose for which He came. He endured not only the physical agony of death by crucifixion, but also the emotional and mental anguish of becoming the sin offering, bearing the sins of the whole world. It was the Father who baptized Jesus into this suffering. Jesus referred to it as the cup His Father had given Him. In Jesus's agony in Gethsemane we hear Him pray to His Father,

"Nevertheless not My will, but Yours, be done" (Luke 22:42). It was the cross of Calvary that was the element used to effect this baptism of suffering as a vicarious, propitiary sacrifice for the salvation of mankind.

Jesus did not exempt His disciples from a similar fiery baptism. When the mother of James and John took her sons to ask Jesus to let them sit, one on the right hand and the other on the left in His kingdom, Jesus said to them, "You do not know what you are asking. Are you able to drink from the cup that I am to drink, and to be baptized with the baptism that I am baptized with?" (Matt. 20:22). When they assured Him they were able, He replied that they would know His baptism, but it was not His to say who would sit with Him in glory. And He taught His disciples, "If anyone wishes to come after Me, he must deny himself, and take up his cross and follow Me" (Matt. 16:24, NAS). A cross is for crucifixion, and that means suffering.

As we surrender to the Christ-life, we find that where the will of God contradicts our wills, there a cross is laid upon our self-lives that causes suffering and death. When our thoughts and desires do not agree with God's, we must choose to deny them. In that denial we find the cross upon which they must die. What should be our attitude in this suffering? We should not become morbid in it. Instead, we should respond as Jesus did, "who for the joy that was set before Him endured the cross" (Heb. 12:2). Although there is death on one side of the cross, there is life on the other, for out of death comes life. Resurrection power awaits us on the other side of the cross. Paul declared this:

> For if we have become united with Him in the likeness
> of His death, certainly we shall be also in the likeness

of His resurrection, knowing this, that our old self was
crucified with Him, in order that our body of sin might
be done away with, so that we should no longer be slaves
to sin.

—Romans 6:5–6, nas

Our suffering brings death to our sin nature, which we
exchange for the nature of Christ in resurrection life. All suffering is not caused by our personal sin. Whatever cross the
Father ordains for us, however, in our personal baptism of
suffering, we must be willing to yield to submissively. It is a
matter of consecration, the giving up of our will, our way, our
walk, our words, our works, our worship, and our warfare in
exchange for His. In this way we will enter into the fellowship
of His sufferings and be transformed into the image of Christ.

UNDERSTANDING THE BAPTISM
OF THE HOLY SPIRIT

Having seen the scriptural pattern of baptisms, we can focus
now on the significance of what it means to be baptized into
the Holy Spirit.[4] We must always keep in mind that we cannot
receive anything from God without the work of the Holy
Spirit. As we have seen, it is the Holy Spirit who convicts us of
sin, washing it away in the blood of the Lamb when we repent.
So He is working in our lives before we are saved to draw us
to God and cause us to recognize our need of Him. It is He
who bears witness in our spirits that we are born-again children of God.

Then, after we are born again, there is an "enduement with
power" that Jesus promised to His disciples. Just before He
ascended into the clouds, Jesus specifically instructed His disciples to wait for the enduement of power they would receive

when the Holy Spirit came. To understand this baptism more fully, it will help us to study the disciples' experience of new birth and their subsequent enduement with power on the Day of Pentecost.

Resurrection morning

The morning that Jesus rose from the dead, Mary Magdalene had gone to His tomb. When she found the tomb empty and had announced her findings to the disciples, they ran to investigate what had happened. After they left, Mary was standing outside the tomb crying, when she saw a man there whom she thought must be the gardener. How sweet must have been her joy when Jesus called her name and she recognized her lovely Savior! As she fell to worship Him, He asked her not to touch Him, saying, "I have not yet ascended to the Father..." (John 20:17, NAS). He couldn't let her touch Him because, as our High Priest, He had to present Himself to the Father as the spotless Lamb slain for our sins.

Jesus came to the earth to fulfill all the law of God. According to that law, the high priest took the blood of the slain lamb into the holiest of holies in the tabernacle. From the time they were cleansed until they went into the holy place, the Old Testament priests were not allowed to be defiled by man. The law said that if the priest was clean when he went into the presence of God with the blood sacrifice, he would live. Otherwise, he would die in the presence of God. When the priest came out of the tabernacle, he declared to the people that their sins were covered for another year. The blood of the lamb had atoned for their sins.

Jesus had prayed His priestly prayer, died, and risen from the dead. But when He saw Mary that morning, He had not yet gone into the heavenly tabernacle as our slain Lamb, so she could not touch Him. He had been cleansed; He was alive; He became the Lamb slain that the Old Testament types had foreshadowed. Never again would there have to be a lamb slain because Jesus became the eternal paschal sacrifice for sin. We know Jesus was accepted in the Father's presence during the first part of resurrection day because He came back to appear to His disciples. Jesus carried His own blood into the presence of God and sprinkled it on the heavenly mercy seat. When He came back that day, He had fulfilled all the types and shadows regarding the atonement.

Until the day of Jesus's death on the cross, everyone had looked forward in time to the coming of the Messiah—every type and shadow pointed to the Lamb of God who would take away the sin of the world. Those who walked in obedience to the law were counted righteous. When Jesus walked on this earth, He was still under the law, and He fulfilled the law by walking in obedience to His Father without sin.

Jesus's supreme sacrifice became the mediatorial, efficacious, vicarious, substitutionary work of redemption. Each of those words explains what happened at Calvary. His dying was mediatorial; He became our mediator before the justice of God. *Efficacious* means it is as effective today as it was the day He died. *Vicarious* and *substitutionary* mean He died in my stead the death I deserved to die. But Jesus didn't complete the redeeming work until He went to heaven, took His blood, and came back as a spiritual being in a glorified body.

Then He appeared on the road to Emmaus and walked with two disciples (not of the twelve disciples), causing their hearts to bum as He opened the Scriptures to them. At the end of that day, as the disciples were in an upper room with the doors locked, Jesus came and stood among them and said, "Peace." He showed them His hands and His side. (See

Luke 24.) The disciples were overjoyed! There was no doubt in their minds that this was their Lord. He could not be an impostor—He had been crucified and now He was alive!

Divine breath

Later Jesus *breathed* on them and said to them, "Receive the Holy Spirit" (John 20:22, NAS). When He breathed on them, He breathed His life into them. Jesus was no longer *with* them; He would now be *in* them. This is what Paul described as "Christ in you, the hope of glory" (Col. 1:27). That was the day the "Jesus" who had walked with and worked through the disciples became "The Christ" of His church through this divine impartation to His disciples. Then, as we shall see, the church was baptized in the Holy Spirit on the Day of Pentecost.

Although some evangelicals teach that the disciples' experience of receiving Jesus's breath was the same as the baptism of the Holy Spirit, it is clear from the Scriptures that the disciples did not receive His baptism here, but His breath. The Greek word used here for breath is *pneuma*. The Greek word for baptism, as we have seen, is *baptizo*. There is a great difference between being breathed upon and being baptized. Although they did receive an impartation of Christ's life when He breathed on them, their baptism in the Holy Spirit was still to come.

Divine blessing

Later, just before His ascension, Jesus led His disciples out to Bethany and blessed them. That blessing is a reality that Jesus gives to all who are born again. In that setting He also gave them the commission to preach the gospel to the whole world.

Divine baptism

It was during these same days before His ascension that Jesus instructed His disciples to wait in Jerusalem, saying, "For John baptized with water, but you shall be baptized with the Holy Spirit not many days from now" (Acts 1:5). This was the promise of the Father of whom Jesus had said, "He lives with you, and will be in you" (John 14:17).

Although people had not been baptized in the Holy Spirit before, He did move *upon* people in the Old Testament. I have found seventeen places in the Scriptures that the Holy Spirit moved upon people. And most, if not all, of the gifts of the Holy Spirit listed in the New Testament operated through these Old Testament saints as well. People who were moved upon by the Holy Spirit prophesied, had words of wisdom, words of knowledge, power to work miracles, and power to heal. The Scriptures declare that the Holy Spirit settled upon them to empower them for these supernatural acts.

Now, in the fullness of time the Father would send the Comforter at Jesus's request. The disciples could expect the Holy Spirit to come on a certain day because He had always fulfilled all of the feast days and oblations. The more we study the precious truths revealed through scriptural types and shadows, the better we understand that God's timing was according to divine pattern. The Holy Spirit would not come any other day but the Day of Pentecost because He *is* Pentecost.

The Day of Pentecost was the second period of the Jewish feast days. The first included the Feast of Unleavened Bread, Feast of Passover, and Feast of Firstfruits—representing the death, burial, and resurrection of our Lord. Jesus had just fulfilled this first period of feasts by His death and resurrection, providing the reality it foreshadowed. Fifty days later in the Jewish calendar, the head of every Jewish family was supposed to come to the temple on Pentecost Day to celebrate the Feast of Pentecost. Since Jesus had been with His disciples for forty days after His resurrection, there were only ten days left before the Feast of Pentecost would arrive.

What a thrilling account Luke gives us of the Holy Spirit's coming! He wrote:

> When the day of Pentecost had come, they were all together in one place. Suddenly a sound like a mighty rushing wind came from heaven, and it filled the whole house where they were sitting. There appeared to them tongues as of fire, being distributed and resting on each of them, and they were all filled with the Holy Spirit and began to speak in other tongues, as the Spirit enabled them to speak.
>
> —ACTS 2:1–4

It was on that day when the disciples and all those in the upper room were baptized in the Holy Spirit that the world first saw the church. The church was baptized on the Day of Pentecost. The disciples were saved before the Day of Pentecost, filled with joy and commissioned by Jesus. Then the church was empowered as Jesus had promised on the Day of Pentecost and displayed to the world.

Two kinds of tongues

Many sincere Christian people have not accepted the reality of the baptism of the Holy Spirit with the initial evidence of speaking in tongues because they have not understood what happened on the Day of Pentecost. Some evangelical denominations teach that the gifts of the Spirit functioned only in the early church and are not functioning today. According to this teaching, the disciples received the *gift* of tongues (as taught in

1 Corinthians 12) on the Day of Pentecost. Because some evangelicals believe that the gifts are not operating in the church today, they teach that believers do not speak in tongues now when they receive the baptism of the Holy Spirit. Some teach that the other spiritual gifts Paul listed for the Corinthians are not necessary for the church today either, although they concede that God could use them if He wanted to, for example, on the mission field as a sign to unbelievers.

Evangelicals also teach that God gave spiritual gifts, such as tongues, to the early church mainly to show there was no difference between the Jews and the Gentiles. They point to passages such as Acts 10, which relates the story of Cornelius and his household of Gentiles who received the Holy Spirit. Those Jews present knew that the Holy Spirit was poured out on the Gentiles because they "heard them speaking in other tongues and magnifying God..." (Acts 10:46). That purpose having been accomplished, there is no need for these gifts to function today, according to those who embrace this theology.

I was trained in this evangelical theology, so I did not accept the fact of tongues as the initial evidence of receiving the baptism of the Holy Spirit. As I studied the Scriptures, however, desiring to know the truth regarding this biblical experience, I went to a Pentecostal preacher to ask him if he could define for me the tongues in the second chapter of Acts. My question was, "Did the disciples speak with a tongue of ecstasy that was the initial evidence of the baptism of the Holy Spirit, as well as the gift of tongues as taught in 1 Corinthians chapter 12?" If there were two kinds of tongues there, I would accept the doctrine of the baptism of the Holy Spirit that is subsequent to regeneration as the Pentecostals teach.

I knew, from studying the Word, that the gift of tongues needed to be interpreted and that it was given to edify and to convince the unbeliever. I also read in Acts that on the Day of Pentecost, men from many nations heard in their own languages the disciples speaking of the glories of God, and three thousand souls were saved. It was obvious to me that the gift of tongues was functioning there. Yet Pentecostals teach that the tongues a person speaks when baptized in the Holy Spirit is unknown to all except God. The conflict in my understanding was I saw the gift of tongues in action on the Day of Pentecost, but did not see the unknown tongues as the initial evidence of the baptism of the Holy Spirit operating that day.

When I asked this Pentecostal minister if he could differentiate the tongues for me in Acts 2, he declared that the gift of tongues was not operating on the Day of Pentecost. I had read Acts too well to accept that. I repeated, "You mean that is not the gift of tongues as listed in 1 Corinthians chapter 12 that was functioning when all nations heard God glorified in their own languages?" He said, "No, the gift of tongues did not function on the Day of Pentecost." His answer discouraged me from accepting the reality of this baptism, for I knew the gift of tongues was functioning that day. Because I thought that the gifts were not for today, I felt that speaking in tongues could not be a part of the baptism of the Holy Spirit.

What I didn't understand had happened on the Day of Pentecost, took me seventeen years to realize. Only then could I receive this experience as God intended it. Since receiving the baptism of the Holy Spirit with the evidence of speaking in tongues, I have been able to help scores of evangelical people receive this wonderful experience because of the light I received from my divine teacher.

Day of Pentecost revisited

What happened that historical day when the Holy Spirit descended upon the disciples? When the drama opens in the second chapter of Acts, it is the Day of Pentecost. It is a feast day of the Jews for which many came to Jerusalem from every nation. These Jews are meeting in the temple. In the upper room something else is happening. Let's open the curtain on the first scene of this drama. There are one hundred twenty people sitting in a little upstairs room. When the Day of Pentecost was fully come, or dawned, the Holy Spirit came to them. The Jewish tradition considered the time of daybreak as six o'clock in the morning. So I believe the Scriptures are specifically stating that the Holy Spirit arrived at six o'clock in the morning, at the dawning of the Day of Pentecost. This fact will become more significant as the drama unfolds.

Now as we watch this scene unfold at daybreak, the Scriptures say, "And suddenly there came from heaven a noise like a violent rushing wind, and it filled the whole house where they were sitting" (Acts 2:2, NAS). The Scriptures clearly state that this was the Holy Spirit coming. And when He came, "there appeared to them tongues as of fire distributing themselves, and they rested on each one of them" (v. 3, NAS).

Each person was filled with the Holy Spirit and began to speak with other tongues as the Spirit was giving them utterance. The Phillips translation renders this tongue, "the tongue of ecstasy," which means "an overflow of something inside that has spilled out." When this supernatural splash took place, one hundred twenty people "overflowed." They were speaking in a language that didn't mean anything to anyone but God. No one understood this ecstatic language of the Spirit. When these one hundred twenty people exploded in an ecstatic expression of praise to God given by the Holy Spirit, it caused a stir in the city that created the next scene of this divine drama.

When the curtain opens on scene two, something has happened in the town. "Now there were Jews living in Jerusalem, devout men from every nation under heaven" (v. 5, NAS). The crowd in the temple was going through the *ritual* of Pentecost, not knowing that the *reality* of Pentecost had come in Person. When they heard the sound from the upper room, "the crowd came together, and were bewildered because each one of them was hearing them speak in his own language" (v. 6, NAS). This multitude is not in the upper room, for there were too many people to have fit into that small area. The people in the upper room have gone out to see the multitude. It is at this time that these Jews from every nation hear the disciples speaking in languages that they can understand.

The tongues the multitude hears are not heaven's language of ecstasy that the disciples received at the dawning of the day. What the multitude hears now in their own languages is called "divers tongues" in the Scriptures, which are tongues specifically given for the unbeliever to hear (1 Cor. 14). The disciples couldn't have spoken in these divers tongues if they had not received the baptism in the Holy Spirit and spoken in tongues of ecstasy, for it is He who gives the gift of tongues. They were baptized in the upper room as "tongues as of fire" sat on each of them. They have been talking to God since the dawning of the morning in tongues of ecstasy, and now God is speaking back through them to the nations in divers tongues.

To show us which nations were there and what languages they spoke, the Scriptures list the nationalities. "Parthians and Medes and Elamites, and residents of Mesopotamia, Judea and Cappadocia, Pontus and Asia, Phrygia and Pamphylia, Egypt and the districts of Libya around Cyrene, and visitors from

Rome, both Jews and proselytes, Cretans and Arabs…" were all present (Acts 2:9–11, NAS). These unbelievers heard messages from God in their own languages supernaturally. God communicated His message to every nation in a matter of a few hours, without the help of television or satellites like we have today.

It is Peter who sets the time period of this scene for us as three hours after the Holy Spirit first came to the disciples in the upper room. When some mocked and said that the disciples were full of sweet wine, Peter stood up and reminded them that people did not drink that early in the day, at nine o'clock in the morning. The Holy Spirit had come when the Day of Pentecost had fully dawned, probably about six o'clock in the morning. So the disciples had spoken in tongues of ecstasy for two or three hours before the "unbelievers" from all those nations showed up. It was when the disciples came to greet the multitude that the Holy Spirit gave them divers tongues to communicate to all the nations represented the glories of God they were experiencing.

That Pentecostal preacher couldn't answer my question, and I spent seventeen years serving God without receiving an answer. I knew the gift of tongues was operating on the Day of Pentecost because I had read how Paul described it to the Corinthians. But I didn't understand that the tongue of ecstasy came to those disciples before the gift of tongues did until a precious saint of God, Rev. Ralph Byrd, walked by me one morning when I was praying, and asked, "What time of day did the disciples get the baptism?"

I replied smartly, "Nine o'clock." He said, "I asked you what time the disciples were baptized." I repeated, "Nine o'clock." He didn't accept my answer. He asked me again, a third time, the same question. I looked at him intently and said, "Daddy

Byrd, I don't know much, but Peter said it was nine o'clock."
He retorted, "I didn't ask you what time Peter said it was."
Then he walked off and left me without explaining anything.
So I got my Bible and began to study and talk to my teacher.
It was then He made me to understand the difference between
the tongues of ecstasy the disciples received at the dawning of
the day, and the gift of tongues that operated through them
for the multitude in the second scene when Peter, defending
them, said it was but nine o'clock in the morning. This understanding dispelled my confusion for I saw that the coming of
the Holy Spirit included the initial baptism of the Holy Spirit
with the one hundred twenty as the day dawned in that small
upper room. Those who had tarried there were "all filled" and
spoke ecstatically in other tongues, glorifying God. Then later
that morning the multitudes came and God gave the disciples
divers tongues to declare the works of God to all the nations,
and three thousand unbelievers were saved.

I have a deep concern for others to be able to differentiate
between the initial evidence of Holy Spirit baptism, where
speaking in tongues is an overflow in a language known only
to God, and the tongue that is interpreted to man and understood, as Paul teaches (1 Cor. 12). We announced in a meeting
recently that people should invite their denominational friends
to come to a special meeting where we would teach concerning
the baptism of the Holy Spirit. We believed that as we taught
the clarity of this truth, they would see and understand. In
that meeting forty-eight people received the baptism of the
Holy Spirit through our simply reading chapter 2 from the
Book of Acts and dividing it into the two scenes of God's
drama on Pentecost Day. When we finished reading, these sincere Christians came to the altar and received the baptism of
the Holy Spirit with the evidence of speaking in tongues.

Why tongues?

Why do we need to speak with tongues as an evidence of receiving the baptism of the Holy Spirit? Perhaps we need to answer this question first: Why were seventeen different nationalities in Jerusalem that day witnessing the phenomena of the disciples glorifying God in their languages? God, in original creation, made one language until men decided to build the tower of Babel and become as God, and so pride entered their hearts. Then God confused their languages and scattered them across the earth. From the time of the building of the tower of Babel to the Day of Pentecost nothing brought men together in one language.

On the Day of Pentecost as the disciples had humbled themselves to wait for the promise of the Father, God had a message for all mankind. He didn't deliver His message through confusion; every man heard it in his language. Now for the first time since Babel the body of Christ can speak the same language, a heavenly one. The language of the Holy Spirit is the only language that is not a part of the curse. It is a language of the heavenly world coming from our spirits by the power of the Holy Spirit.

This tongue of ecstasy is also our heavenly prayer language that no one but God understands. That is why it is called an unknown tongue. No one has to interpret it as is required for the gift of tongues. The believer soon realizes that the world, the flesh, and the devil are his three enemies. The only time we speak without these enemies knowing a word we say is when we speak in an unknown tongue. It becomes our private line to God that gives us direct access to Him. We pick up that heavenly "telephone" and call heaven, and the devil doesn't know a word we are saying. The world and flesh don't know that language; that is the reason they hate it.

However, when the Holy Spirit prays to God out of our spirits in His heavenly language, He will, if we ask Him, give back through our minds the revelation of what He prayed to God about or for us. As we yield to the Holy Spirit within, out will flow worship, ecstasy, and joy. We can sing to Him, shout to Him, and pray to Him in that tongue of ecstasy that overflows. Only God the Father, Jesus, and the Holy Spirit know what we are saying as we pray in that heavenly language.

As we speak to God in the language of the Spirit, Paul said we are edified as our spirits pray. He declared that he would pray and sing in the spirit as well as with his understanding (1 Cor. 14:14–15). Although he gave specific instructions for the use of tongues in a public service, he in no way meant to deny the reality or power they exert in a believer's life. He even declared that he spoke in tongues more than all of them (v. 18). In his letter to the Corinthians he was simply correcting the problem of tongues being misused in public services in a way that was creating confusion.

After receiving the baptism of the Holy Spirit, I understood that the gifts of the Spirit were for today as well. There is nothing in the Scriptures to indicate otherwise, for these gifts are given to edify the church. As we allow the Holy Spirit to fill us continually, we will gain greater understanding of the gifts of the Holy Spirit.

Chapter 3

Gifts of the Holy Spirit

Part I:
Divine Enablement to Know

. . . .

Now concerning spiritual gifts, brothers, I do not want you to be ignorant.... There are various gifts, but the same Spirit. There are differences of administrations, but the same Lord. There are various operations, but it is the same God who operates all of them in all people. But the manifestation of the Spirit is given to everyone for the common good.

—1 Corinthians 12:1–7

. . . .

Honor in the Godhead

ALTHOUGH MANY CHRISTIANS have referred to the Holy Spirit as an "it," or gifts, or tongues, and some believe He is merely an influence, He is none of these. He is a divine Person, the third Person of the Godhead. The Scriptures are full of affirmations of this truth, giving the Holy Spirit at least forty different titles and listing at least twenty-seven attributes of His divine personality. (See Appendix A.)

Therefore, we should attribute as much honor to God the Holy Spirit as we do to God the Father and God the Son. In order to properly evaluate the work of the Holy Spirit, it seems very important that we should closely observe how the three members of the Godhead have been at marked pains to provide for the honor of the other. We should be as careful to give each of Them that honor as They are.

How careful the Father was to guard the glory of His beloved Son when the Son laid aside the visible insignia of His deity and took upon Himself the form of a servant. The Father's voice was then heard more than once proclaiming, "This is My beloved Son." Then how constantly did the incarnate Son revert attention from Himself and direct it to the Father who had sent Him, saying, "...The Son can do nothing of Himself, but what He sees the Father do..." (John 5:19). In like manner the Holy Spirit is not here to glorify Himself but to exalt Jesus, whose advocate He is.

Blessed is it then to mark how jealous both the Father and the Son have been to safeguard the glory and provide for the honor due the Holy Spirit, as we shall learn from our study. Although this blessed Trinity is one God, the Scriptures reveal Them to us as three parts of the Triune Godhead, perfect in unity yet differing in function. Thus each one of the Persons of the Trinity is careful to provide for the honor of the others. Accepting this spiritual reality will prevent us from dishonoring the Holy Spirit by being critical of His gifts and manifestations, and will help us to properly evaluate His divine work in the earth.

COMING OF CHRIST AND OF THE
HOLY SPIRIT PARALLELED

Many and marked are the parallels between the coming of Christ and the coming of the Holy Spirit. The coming of both Christ and the Holy Spirit were subject to Old Testament prediction. During the past century theologians have written much about Messianic prophecy. But unfortunately the promises that God gave concerning the coming of the Holy Spirit have seemed vague to many people. Yet the prophets definitely predicted the descent of the Holy Spirit (Joel 2:28) as well as the incarnation of the Savior (Isa. 7:14).

Just as Christ had John the Baptist announce His incarnation and prepare His way, so the Holy Spirit had Christ Himself to foretell His coming and to make ready the hearts of His disciples. Just as it was not until the fullness of time had come that God sent forth His Son, so it was not until the Day of Pentecost was fully come that God sent forth His Spirit. As the Son became incarnate in the holy land of Palestine, so the Spirit descended in Jerusalem.

Just as the coming of the Son of God into the world was accompanied by mighty wonders and signs, so the descent of God's Spirit was attended by dramatic displays of divine power. The advent of each was marked by supernatural phenomena. The angelic host announcing Jesus's birth found its counterpart in the "sound from heaven as of a rushing mighty wind" (Acts 2:2, KJV) announcing the coming of the Holy Spirit. As an extraordinary star marked the house where the child was, so a divine sound of rushing wind and cloven tongues of fire marked the house where the Spirit came.

Concerning the coming of Jesus, there was both a private and public aspect to it. The birth of the Savior was made known unto a few. But when Jesus was to be made manifest to Israel, He was publicly identified. At His baptism the heavens opened, the Spirit descended as a dove, and the Father spoke from heaven. Correspondingly, the Spirit was given to the disciples privately when the risen Savior breathed His life into them and said, "Receive the Holy Spirit" (John 20:22, NAS). Not until the Day of Pentecost did the Holy Spirit become public, when the disciples received His baptism. All the multitude in Jerusalem was then made aware of His descent when it was noised abroad.

The advent of the Son was for the purpose of the eternal Word becoming incarnate, made flesh to dwell among us. So too the coming of the Spirit was for the purpose of His becoming incarnate in our flesh. Jesus declared to the disciples that the Spirit of Truth would come and dwell *in* them (John 14:17). The third Person of the Trinity came to take up His abode in man, to whom it is said, "Do you not know that you are the temple of God, and that the Spirit of God dwells in you?" (1 Cor. 3:16)

When Christ was born into the world, we are told that Herod was troubled, and all Jerusalem with Him. In like manner when the Holy Spirit was given, we read, "Now when this was noised abroad, the multitude came together, and were confounded" (Acts 2:6, KJV). It was prophesied that when Christ should appear, He would be unrecognized and unappreciated. So it came to pass. In like manner, the Lord Jesus declared He would send the Spirit of Truth, "whom the world cannot receive, for it does not see Him, neither does it know Him" (John 14:17).

As the Messianic claims of Christ were called into question, so the advent of the Spirit was at once challenged. We read that on the Day of Pentecost the multitude "all continued in amazement and great perplexity, saying to one another, 'What does this mean?'" (Acts 2:12, NAS). The analogy is yet closer, for as Christ was termed a wine-bibber, so of those filled with the Spirit some of the multitude "were mocking and saying, 'They are full of sweet wine'" (v. 13, NAS). Also, as the public coming of Christ was heralded by John the Baptist, so the public descent of the Spirit was interpreted by Peter.

God appointed unto Christ the execution of the all-inclusive work of redeeming us from Satan's interruption of our Father's eternal plan for mankind, and reproducing His divine character in mankind. Even so the Spirit has been assigned the momentous task of effectually applying the virtues of the atonement and restoring believers to the image of God through the impartation of His character. As the Son honored the Father in the fulfillment of His eternal purpose, so the Holy Spirit glorifies the Son in the fulfillment of His divine mission. The Father paid holy deference to the Son by bidding the disciples, "Listen to Him" (Matt. 17:5). In like manner the Son showed that respect to our teacher when He said, "He who has an ear, let him hear what the Spirit says to the churches" (Rev. 2:29). And as Christ committed His saints to the safekeeping of the Holy Spirit, so the Spirit will yet deliver us in safety at the return of Jesus (John 14:3).

These interesting parallels give insight into the comprehensive love of God for mankind, as well as show the honor and love that exists between the members of the Godhead. May our hearts be enlarged through this understanding to grasp the true significance of the work of the Holy Spirit in the earth. His is an eternal mandate to bring complete redemption to lost mankind for all who will choose to know Him. With this perspective, we can better understand the importance of spiritual gifts and how to give them their rightful place in our lives and churches.

PURPOSE OF THE SPIRITUAL GIFTS

A complete presentation of the Holy Spirit cannot be made without a thorough discussion of spiritual gifts. There are approximately one hundred New Testament references to the subject of spiritual gifts, or to the exercise of those gifts that are listed in chapter 12 of 1 Corinthians. (This number is exclusive of the miracles of Jesus recorded in the Gospels.)

In spite of these frequent references in Scripture to the manifestation of the gifts of the Spirit in the New Testament church, most of our theology books seem to ignore spiritual gifts. If they include a paragraph or two, it is usually with the inference that spiritual gifts ceased to function in the church after the apostolic age. There is not the slightest suggestion in the New Testament that any endowment of the Spirit will cease before Jesus returns. On the contrary, the Word declares that the gifts and callings of God are without repentance (Rom. 11:29), which in the Greek means *irrevocable*. With that in mind let's consider the significance of spiritual gifts for the church today.

Spiritual gifts defined

Spiritual gifts are not latent human talents or trained abilities brought to heightened expression. The *pneumatic charismata* are not simply more of what is already resident in men, displayed in excellence. Neither are they enhancements of human personality. They are *the manifestation of the miraculous working of our Lord wrought by the Holy Spirit*. The Holy

Spirit is the channel for the operation of these supernatural gifts, whether seemingly ordinary or seemingly extraordinary.

The nature of the spiritual gifts can be determined largely by the vocabulary used in the Scriptures to refer to them. The first clear reference to the gifts as a supernatural phenomena is found in 1 Corinthians 12, verses 1 through 7. These verses deal with the gifts as a class and provide a vocabulary for their description. They are called *spirituals*, translated from the Greek word *pneumatica*. Paul literally wrote, "Now concerning spiritual *gifts*, brethren, I do not want you to be ignorant" (1 Cor. 12:1, NKJV). The word *gifts* in that verse is in italics, meaning that it is not found in the original Greek manuscript. The first reference to this phenomena classifies them merely as spirituals, or "things of the spirit." The same description is used in 1 Corinthians 14:1. This reference is probably to the gifts, although in 1 Corinthians 14:28, this word *pneumaticos*, in the masculine gender, is applied to "spiritual persons." F. F. Bruce, in his commentary on the Book of First Corinthians, states that *pneumatica* is referring to the persons "endowed with spiritual gifts." So the spirituals in one sense refer to gifts and in another refer to persons having spiritual gifts.

Spiritual gifts, *charismata*, include diversities of gifts (1 Cor. 12:4). The Greek word *charisma*, which means "spiritual gifts," comes from the basic word *charis*, which means grace. Charisma is a divine enablement, an endowment, or grace bestowed freely by God. The text in 1 Corinthians refers to the gifts as spirituals because they are *capacities freely bestowed by the Holy Spirit*. They cannot be merited, bought, or earned for they are of divine origin. They operate through a Spirit-filled person, but in a real sense they are gifts to the church, to the whole body of Christ. The apostle Paul explains this diversity and the necessity of each member of the body of

Christ functioning properly, using the analogy of the human body (1 Cor. 12:12–27). Each manifestation of the Spirit is for the common good of the church. So when the Holy Spirit manifests Himself through a divine gift operating through a believer, its purpose is to reveal and glorify Jesus for the profit of the corporate body of Christ. This includes ministry either to one person, to several, or to a whole body, as the Lord moves supernaturally to meet the needs of His people.

Proper motivation: love

When instructing the church concerning the use of spiritual gifts, Paul said, "Let all things be done for edification" (1 Cor. 14:26). The words *edify* and *profit* are used eight times in Paul's first letter to the Corinthians with relation to the operation of these gifts. If a spiritual gift is exercised without the proper motivation of love, it will not edify the body and will therefore be unprofitable. Whatever the manifestation of the Spirit, its only purpose is to build and strengthen the unique structure that is Christ's church. Any exercise of the spiritual gifts that does not result in edifying the body of Christ and glorifying Jesus is out of order. Then test of the validity of exercising a gift is the benefit it brings to the community of believers.

As part of Paul's exhortation to the Corinthians to desire the best gifts, he tells them also to follow the way of love. Many different kinds of gifts are named and listed throughout the letters to the Corinthians and the Romans. However, love is not listed as a gift (see diagram).[1]

Some teach erroneously that love is the greatest gift. However, love is not a gift; *it is the way by which we are to be guided and motivated.* Paul interrupted his discourse on spiritual gifts to declare with urgency that all the charismas must

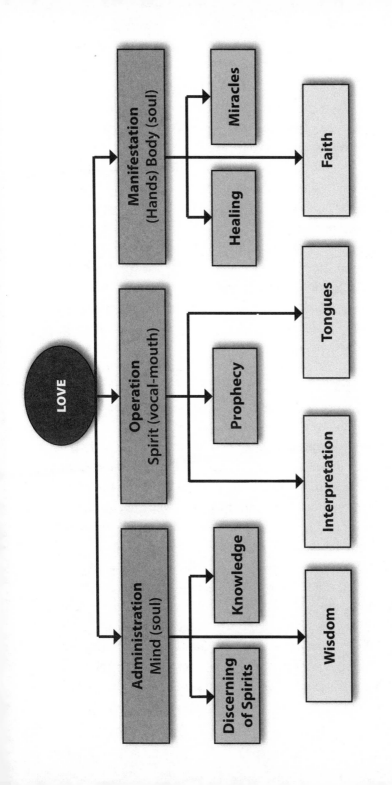

be exercised through love. He declared that the person who exercises gifts without love becomes nothing and gains nothing.

It is a tragedy that some individuals who have been blessed with spiritual gifts have become nothing in the eyes of God because they lack compassion, patience, kindness, long-suffering, and other attributes of love (1 Cor. 13). Love should always be the motivation for seeking and the way of expressing each of the spiritual gifts. If love is truly present in the church that is manifesting spiritual gifts, those gifts can have a tremendous impact, bringing God's power and presence. When the gifts of the Spirit are infused with the love of God, the body of Christ is blessed and, in turn, becomes a blessing to others.

Because of the great value the spiritual gifts have in building the body of Christ, believers should desire them. The apostle Paul encourages the Corinthians to eagerly desire spiritual gifts (1 Cor. 14:1). This is by no means a self-oriented desire for personal blessing. As noted before, the purpose of the gifts is to reveal Jesus and to edify the body of Christ. For that reason the spiritual gifts are to be earnestly desired. The whole body of believers should desire all the gifts of the Spirit to be manifested, not just a few of them. Through variety of expression, multiple needs are met. The whole fellowship of believers is built up by seeing the unveiled beauty of our Lord through the supernatural expressions of the gifts.

To be sure, the Holy Spirit distributes spiritual gifts as He wills, but this is not without regard to the desires of those members of the body of Christ who wish to be used by the Holy Spirit. Concerning this Christ-focused ministry, each person has a distinctive role to fulfill. To each one is given the manifestation of the Spirit, and each person in the local church can be involved in that expression. Believers should not look to one person or to a few to minister in the gifts in a local church. Rather, they should look to the Lord, expecting Him to minister by His Spirit through all who are present. Of course, this calls for individual responsibility of a high order. This means that believers should closely follow the leading and prompting of the Holy Spirit, and whenever He exercises a gift it should be brought forth in harmony and proper order.

As we consider individually the spirituals listed in chapter 12 of 1 Corinthians, we will continue to discover the goodness of God in giving gifts to His church. Studying these nine gifts separately, we will better understand how each can be used for the edifying and building of the body of Christ. Also, we will learn the safeguards the Scriptures give us to maintain the valid manifestation of these powerful spiritual gifts.

Words of Wisdom and Knowledge

> To one is given by the Spirit the word of wisdom, to another the word of knowledge by the same Spirit.
> —1 Corinthians 12:8

The Greek term in this verse translated "word" is *logos*. It is a common New Testament term that is also translated as "utterance" or "message." These two *logos* gifts—the word of wisdom and the word of knowledge—head a list of nine diverse ways in which the Spirit is manifested for the common good of the body of Christ (1 Cor. 12:7). Traditionally these two gifts have been understood differently by various parts of the body of Christ.

One of the ways charismatic believers define the word of knowledge is "a supernatural insight that gives a Spirit-filled believer specific information about a person and situation, spontaneously revealed to him by the Holy Spirit." According to this popular understanding, a word of knowledge is a mental impression, a picture, or vision through which the Holy Spirit discloses some hidden fact or circumstance concerning people, places, or things. Similarly, a word of wisdom, according to this view, is a spontaneous revelation of wise guidance or knowledge rightly applied. Although these are legitimate definitions of the function of these two spiritual gifts, they are not the only way the Scriptures define them.

The Scriptures also refer to these two kindred manifestations of the Spirit as "gifts of speaking." According to this definition, these gifts function as "spontaneous revelation of divine truth from the Word of God spoken forth." Thus, teaching and preaching under the anointing of the Holy Spirit that includes speaking forth divine revelation is also a manifestation of these revelatory gifts. It is my conviction that this is the greater manifestation of the gifts of word of wisdom and knowledge.

We would wonder why Paul began his discussion of these nine spirituals with the words of wisdom and knowledge. In all likelihood it was because wisdom (*sophia*) and knowledge (*kenosis*) were watchwords of the Corinthian church, a Greek congregation that was fascinated with human philosophy and the gift of oratory. The language Paul used here apparently referred back to the problems that he addressed in the first chapter of this book (1 Cor. 1:17–2:16), in which he denounced worldly philosophy expressed in empty human eloquence. In the early sections of his letter to the Corinthians Paul had much to say on the subject of wisdom. (He referred to "wisdom" or "wise" twenty times in the first two chapters and mentioned "knowledge" or "know" sixteen times in the first eight chapters.) The Greek word Paul used for *knowing* referred to intimate relationship through the revelation of the mind of Christ. At issue was the Corinthians' emphasis of speaking through humanly attained wisdom and knowledge, a practice that contradicted Paul's Spirit-empowered preaching of the cross.

Rejecting the common criteria for spirituality according to the Corinthians, Paul declares that Christ sent him to preach the gospel, not with words of human wisdom, lest the cross of Christ be emptied of its power (1 Cor. 1:17). He wrote:

> And when I came to you, brethren, I did not come with superiority of speech or of wisdom, proclaiming to you the testimony of God. For I determined to know nothing among you except Jesus Christ, and Him crucified....And my message and my preaching were not in persuasive words of wisdom, but in demonstration of the Spirit and of power, so that your faith would not rest on the wisdom of men, but on the power of God.
>
> —1 CORINTHIANS 2:1–2, 4–5, NAS

Paul implied that the *words*, translated from *logos*, of his message were not of human origin, or mere philosophical speculation. Instead, his message came from another source: the Holy Spirit. Not only were his words accompanied by convincing proof of God's power (undoubtedly signs and wonders), but the message itself was a powerful demonstration of the Spirit's presence (1 Cor. 2:4). Then, in discussing the spiritual gifts, Paul used the Corinthians' own special terms to begin his list (1 Cor. 12:8). In this way he reduced words of wisdom and knowledge from the Corinthians' fascination with human abilities, and the arrogance it produced, to true revelation by the Holy Spirit.

Words of wisdom and knowledge are probably best understood in Paul's explanation in the following words: "But God has revealed them to us by His Spirit. For the Spirit searches all things, yes, the deep things of God" (1 Cor. 2:10). These gifts function through a revelation of God Himself. The Holy Spirit plumbs the "deep things" of God, searches out His profound thoughts, breathes on them, and lifes them to believers' hearts through revelation. Those believers who receive such revelation will be able to proclaim that revelation to others and see them lifed by the word as well. The words of such a message, although framed by the mind of the speaker, spring from a higher source. That is what Paul meant when he wrote, "Which things also we speak, not in the words which man's wisdom teacheth, but which the Holy Ghost teacheth…" (1 Cor. 2:13, KJV). A person who so speaks will not depend on previous training, human wisdom, or eloquence, but on the power and the inspiration of the Holy Spirit.

Thus, a word of wisdom has as its source Christ Jesus, "whom of God made unto us wisdom, righteousness, sanctification, and redemption" (1 Cor. 1:30). Paul explained that he spoke God's wisdom "in a mystery, the hidden wisdom, which God predestined before the ages to our glory" (1 Cor. 2:7, NAS). God's wise plan of redemption was secret and mysterious in the sense that it was hidden in God from all human eyes. But it is now manifest in Christ and revealed through the Holy Spirit. Yet God's wisdom remains hidden to those who consider the message of the cross foolishness (1 Cor. 1:18; 2:14), not understanding God's eternal purpose.

The primary and authoritative revelation of God's secret wisdom and eternal purpose was given to Paul (1 Cor. 4:1) and to other apostles and prophets (Eph. 3:3–6), that now it might be made known unto the church. According to these Scriptures, insight into divine wisdom was given as a spiritual gift and spoken forth to the entire body of Christ through these apostles and prophets (1 Cor. 12:8). This concurs with what we have said, that a word of wisdom may be a special impartation to a particular person preaching a message given by the Holy Spirit. The Holy Spirit enables that person to declare divine truth in a way that transcends his or her natural capacity or experience. We call this "preaching by revelation." If it contains predictive revelation, we classify it as prophetic.

Paul links wisdom and knowledge when writing to the Romans (Rom. 11:33) and to the Colossians (Col. 2:3). His understanding of the manifestation of the gifts of the Spirit is sometimes difficult to determine. Yet there is some biblical evidence that suggests that the two gifts are complementary: the word of wisdom, a preaching gift expressing a message of God's plan of redemption; and the word of knowledge, a teaching gift expressing a message of particular outworking of that plan. Paul writes:

> Now we have received, not the spirit of the world, but the Spirit who is from God, so that we may know the things freely given to us by God which things we also speak, not in words taught by human wisdom, but in those taught by the Spirit, combining spiritual thoughts with spiritual words.
> —1 Corinthians 2:12–13, nas

Here he refers to "knowing things." Perhaps this is a reference to the wide range of blessings that God has graciously bestowed on us in Christ. Out of the knowledge of these things, in words taught by the Holy Spirit, we then speak. This again suggests that a word of knowledge comes forth as teaching or in giving direction for the application of the wisdom spoken.

As we mentioned, the idea that words of wisdom and knowledge should be viewed as speaking gifts, though common among evangelical scholars, is not the popular understanding among charismatic believers. When first introduced to this view, the question is raised, "Does accepting this view make us lose the spontaneous revelatory gifts that we presently call word of wisdom and word of knowledge?" No, they would simply be redefined as prophecy.

In the Scriptures when people reported spontaneous insight the Holy Spirit had given them, Paul called it prophecy. He wrote:

> But if all prophesy and there comes in one who does not believe or one unlearned, he is convinced by all and judged by all. Thus the secrets of his heart are revealed. And so falling down on his face, he will worship God and report that God is truly among you.
>
> —1 Corinthians 14:24–25

Although many charismatic believers would say that when secrets of the heart are manifest the words of knowledge and wisdom are functioning, Paul here includes that phenomenon in prophecy. This is true also of writers in both the Old and New Testaments who considered supernaturally revealed information through words, visions, or dreams a prophetic revelation. For example, David's sin with Bathsheba was revealed to the prophet Nathan (2 Sam. 12:1–12). The battle plans for the Assyrians were revealed to the prophet Elisha (2 Kings 6:8–12). The interpretation of King Nebuchadnezzar's dream was revealed to Daniel in a night vision (Dan. 2:19).

In the New Testament it was through the gift of prophecy that the Holy Spirit revealed that a famine would occur around the world (Acts 11:28), that Paul would be taken captive in Jerusalem (Acts 21:10–11), and that a specific spiritual gift would be given to Timothy (1 Tim. 4:14). When Jesus told a Samaritan woman some specific details about her life, she said, "Sir, I perceive that You are a prophet" (John 4:19). It was because the secrets of her life were revealed that she called Jesus a prophet. As we study the gift of prophecy in more depth in a later chapter, we will understand its purpose more clearly. We are simply contrasting it here with the revelation gifts of wisdom and knowledge to understand more clearly the definition and function of each.

The revelatory gifts of wisdom and knowledge can have tremendous impact in building the church as they supply understanding of the will and purpose of God in various situations. They are so necessary for the impartation of present spiritual truths from the Word of God. Everyone who ministers the Word of God needs to wait on God and earnestly desire the prophetic revelation of His Word in order to be effective in his or her ministry. Only then will we keep in step with the Holy Spirit as He leads the church.

Spirit of wisdom and knowledge

In his letter to the Ephesians, the Holy Spirit through Paul prayed that they might receive a spirit of wisdom and revelation in the knowledge of Him (Eph. 1:17). The stated purpose for that revelation is that they may know "what is the hope of His calling and what are the riches of the glory of His inheritance in the saints" (Eph. 1:18). This was not only Paul's prayer for the church at Ephesus, but also the Holy Spirit's prayer for all "the faithful in Christ Jesus" (Eph. 1:1). That includes the church today.

This prayer is not for just a word of wisdom or a word of knowledge, but also for the spirit of wisdom and knowledge to be ours as well. If we are faithful, we can be recipients of this divine spirit of wisdom and revelation in the knowledge of God and His purposes for His church. I believe the hour has come when we will no longer have to depend only on a word of wisdom or a word of knowledge, but will receive the spirit of wisdom and the spirit of knowledge as we give the Holy Spirit His proper authority in the church.

DISCERNING OF SPIRITS

…to another discerning of spirits…
—I CORINTHIANS 12:10

The gift of discerning of spirits completes the cycle of the revelatory gifts of the Spirit. There is nothing that God knows that may not be made known to man, as the Holy Spirit wills, through the agency of one or more of these three gifts. Everything within the realm of human destiny, whether divine or evil, natural or supernatural, past, present, or future, comes within the parameters of these three revelatory gifts.

The biblical phrase, "discerning of spirits," comes from the Greek word *deakreisis*, and is defined as a verb: "to discern, to discriminate, or to distinguish." This verb form (used in Hebrews 5:14) speaks of those "who by reason of use have their senses exercised to discern both good and evil" (KJV). Paul used this word when questioning whether there was anyone wise enough to judge between the brethren, as to which was right in a certain dispute (1 Cor. 6:5). He used it also to reproach the Corinthian brethren who had not discerned the Lord's body, failing to understand what communion meant (1 Cor. 11:29).

Later in that same book when Paul was setting the gifts in order, he said that the prophets should speak two or three, and let the other judge or discern (1 Cor. 14:29). This seems to infer that someone present should be able to discern the validity of the gift of prophecy when it is manifested. All Spirit-filled believers are able to judge vocal gifts and their operations in a measure, on the basis of whether they are spiritually edifying to the body. However, when the gift of discerning of spirits is operating, spiritual discernment will be more accurate and effective.

The discerning of spirits is not keen mental penetration or the revelation of people's character or thoughts as through a kind of mental telepathy. It is not psychological insight, nor the critical ability to discover faults in others. Neither is it a supernatural power that operates by the will of man, for all God-given spiritual gifts operate only through the will of the Holy Spirit. There are supernatural powers that operate through the will of man. Such forces as clairvoyance, hypnotism, magic, witchcraft, cultism, sorcery, and spiritualism, though real supernatural forces, are satanic in their origin and operate through the perverted will of man.

The Scriptures indicate quite clearly that the gift of discerning of spirits is the God-given ability to discern the source of a spiritual manifestation, whether it is the Holy Spirit, an evil spirit, or merely the human spirit. It is important to remember that the gift of discerning of spirits is not for the purpose of judging people, but for judging the kind of spirit behind the manifestation, to determine whether it is holy, evil, or human. The gift of discerning of spirits enables the believer to recognize the spirit that has evidenced itself in supernatural power over human bodies, minds, or organs.

Discerning of spirits does not deal exclusively with demon spirits, but allows a person to see God's angels at work as well. It can reveal God's protective angel forces as Elisha the prophet saw them (2 Kings 6:16–17). This gift enabled Stephen to see the Lord just before his martyr's death (Acts 7:55–56), and allowed John to see Him when in exile on the isle of Patmos (Rev. 1:10–16). It often enables believers to see Christ Jesus in the midst of worshippers.

Discerning of spirits enables the possessor of this gift to see through all outward appearances and know the true nature of a situation or the source of an inspired utterance. Seducing spirits or lying spirits are responsible for doctrines of devils and damnable heresy in the church (1 Tim. 4:1–2; 2 Pet. 2:1). The gift of discerning of spirits can discover the enemy's plan of seduction and can unmask demon miracle workers (Rev. 16:14). The Scriptures admonish believers to "test the spirits to see whether they are from God, because many false prophets have gone out into the world" (1 John 4:1). It is vital for the health of the church that we be able to discern correctly the spirits that are influencing believers.

Chapter 4

Gifts of the Holy Spirit

Part II:
Divine Enablement to Do

. . . .

[Jesus] said to them, "Go into all the world, and preach
the gospel to every creature. He who believes and is baptized will be saved. But he who does not believe will
be condemned. These signs will accompany those who
believe: In My name they will cast out demons; they
will speak with new tongues; they will take up serpents;
if they drink any deadly thing, it will not hurt them;
they will lay hands on the sick, and they will recover."

—MARK 16:15–20

. . . .

GIFT OF FAITH

To another faith by the same Spirit…
—1 CORINTHIANS 12:9

IN THIS CHAPTER I want to introduce the three gifts that
enable us to *do* supernaturally: faith, healings, and miracles. God imparts by His Spirit not only understanding, but

also ability. It is insufficient to know; we must also be empowered to do. Of the three gifts of power, faith is undoubtedly the greatest. One writer expressed the power of faith this way: "From Paradise to Patmos, faith marks the trail of the company of the blessed, the heaven-bound, happy-hearted pleasers of God."[1]

The gift of faith is *a supernatural impartation of faith by the Holy Spirit whereby that which is desired by God and spoken by man shall come to pass.* It projects into the eternal realm to bring a supernatural solution into an earthly situation. The gift of faith is given to produce heavenly miracles this side of heaven. Although it is distinct from the working of miracles, as we shall see, it produces them nevertheless. However, receiving the gift of faith does not make it impossible for its possessor to doubt God anymore. Nor does the gift of faith fit a man for heaven any more than speaking with other tongues or any other spiritual gift does. It simply operates by the will of the Spirit through a yielded vessel to bring the will of God to a given situation.

The gift of faith does not include or substitute for all other faith that is taught in the Scriptures. For example, it is distinct from the saving faith that comes before salvation as a gift from God (Eph. 2:8). The gift of faith can be received only after salvation, which is true of all the other spiritual gifts as well.

Faith is the only gift of the Spirit to be included in the list of the fruit of the Spirit (Gal. 5:22–23). This fact reveals to us the necessity of every believer having a quality of faith that grows and develops in order to live fruitful lives. Though all believers may not have the gift of faith operating in their lives, we must all allow that fruit of faith to grow in our lives. The fruit of faith is for character; the gift is for power. Fruit grows, while a gift is a sudden endowment.

The gift of faith differs from other realms of faith, then, as a specific manifestation of supernatural faith given by the Holy Spirit to accomplish a specific purpose. In its operation the element of danger is often the catalyst that triggers the gift of faith. It gave personal protection in perilous circumstances, such as when Daniel was thrown into the lion's den (Dan. 6:17–23), and to the three Hebrew children thrown into the fiery furnace (Dan. 3:16–18). It was used for supernatural sustenance in famine or fasting, as in the case of Elijah and the widow's meal barrel (1 Kings 17:12–16). It was used for supernatural victory in the fight against Amalek (Exod. 17:11), and to assist in domestic and industrial problems, as when the widow's oil was multiplied to pay her debt (2 Kings 4:1–7). The gift of faith was used to receive the astounding promises of God, as when Abraham received his son Isaac miraculously (Rom. 4:20). It was used to raise the dead and cast out evil spirits as well.

Through the gift of faith, God reveals His will and gives power to believe it in the face of impossible circumstances. The Holy Spirit may speak His will to a person through an inner voice or through a vision, and then give a sense of certainty that what has been revealed must happen. We call this knowledge a *rhema* from God—a living word. *Infusion* is a term that best describes the dynamic at work in the gift of faith. Besides revealing His immediate will through a *rhema*, a vision, or an inner voice, God also gives a divine deposit of peace, power, and confidence. This faith is an eternal knowledge imparted to a person that declares an act of God is coming to pass as the spoken words proclaim.

The beautiful chronicle of acts of faith given to us in the Book of Hebrews (chapter 11) teaches us that all divine action is an expression of faith. It was by faith that the elders obtained a good report, and by faith that we under-stand the worlds were framed by the Word of God. By faith Abel offered unto God a more acceptable sacrifice than Cain, and by faith Enoch was translated. Noah and his household were saved by faith, and Abraham answered the call of God by faith. Although we cannot chronicle here all the heroes of faith listed for us in the Scriptures, we mention some to show that as the Scriptures teach, "without faith it is impossible to please God" (Heb. 11:6). God's work will only be accom-plished through acts of faith.

Although this gift is a wonderful manifestation of the power of God given to help the church, we must include here a word of caution regarding its proper use. The whole dynamic involved in the gift of faith is significantly different from a person deciding he or she wants something to happen and therefore speaks according to that desire, claiming it as reality by the mere speaking of it. In the operation of the gift of faith, God initiates the action and our words simply acknowledge what He is revealing and doing, making His will a present reality. Presumption, based on human desire that calls on God to fulfill it, is a dangerous counterfeit to the operation of the gift of faith.

GIFTS OF HEALING

…to another the gifts of healing by the same Spirit.
—1 CORINTHIANS 12:9

Sickness is definitely a result of the fall of man—of original sin. There would have been no sickness on earth had there been no sin (Gen. 2:17; Rom. 5:12). This does not mean, how-ever, that when a person is sick, it is because he or she has sinned. Sickness is not necessarily the result of personal sin, but of sin being in the world. The good news of the gospel is that Jesus has provided healing as part of redemption, the remedy for sin.

The gifts of healing are supernatural manifestations of the Holy Spirit in the sphere of disease, given to the church for the purpose of removing all manner of sickness and infirmities. These gifts bring supernatural healing without the use of natural means of any kind. They are the miraculous manifestation of the Spirit for the banishment of all human ills, whether organic, functional, nervous, acute, or chronic. They must not be confused with the services of the medical profession or the power of mind over matter. Whatever difficulties writers have discovered in defining other gifts of the Spirit, this particular gift seems to be understood by all.

The Scriptures teach many purposes for the gifts of healing that demonstrate the love of God for mankind. (See Appendix B.) These gifts may operate in various ways: through a word, by the laying on of hands, a shadow passing by as with Peter, and even a piece of fabric, as in Paul's ministry. The anointing with oil that James teaches, however, is not the operation of the gifts of healing (James 5:14), but an obedient response to the Word.

Someone frequently used by God in the gifts of healing sees healings take place regularly, often, quickly, progressively, and sometimes dramatically. This spiritual gift is not earned, learned, or purchased. But, oh, what marvelous things happen when the Holy Spirit operates through a human vessel for healing! Temporary and terminal illnesses are healed. The afflicted, lame, and infirmed are made whole. Mental and emotional problems are cured.

As vessels through which this gift is manifest, we need to remember that healing is not a result of our ability but of our

availability. It is always God's supernatural ability working
through our availability that brings healing. Often this gift is
ministered by the laying on of hands as the Scriptures teach.
Some people experience a sensation of the transfer of power
such as an electrical current or surge of warmth flowing when
they minister this gift to a sick person. Sometimes the healing
occurs through a Spirit-prompted word of authority or a command directed to the pressing disease. Often healing comes
through a simple, specific prayer after a time of counseling.

Plurality in healing

The apostle Paul, when listing the spiritual gifts, literally
speaks of gifts of healings (1 Cor. 12:9). This plural form suggests that different kinds of illnesses require diverse types of
healing, implying there may be subcategories of this gift. We
could perhaps relate it to the idea of general practitioners and
specialists in the medical profession. During the years I have
been involved in ministry, I have seen that some can minister
healing effectively to those with the same problems from which
they have been healed, but not as effectively in other situations.
For example, I have seen those who have been healed themselves from stuttering who have an effective ministry of healing
to those who stutter. Some who have had limbs straightened
specialize in praying for those who have crooked limbs. You
might ask why this happens. I believe the Holy Spirit distributes different gifts of healing among believers to keep us
humble and dependent on God and one another.

Some scholars teach that the plural listings of the gifts of
healings may be used to show that this manifestation of the
Holy Spirit has several divine operations. Just as there are
classes of diseases, so each of the gifts of healing probably has
a counteracting effect on some particular disease class. Some

people are greatly used in healing cancers and tumors. Others seem to be empowered to restore sight or hearing. Also, as said before, quite frequently the person has himself been healed of the malady for which he now seems gifted to heal others. Other scholars point out that it is not a stationary gift for a person to use, which is true also for all the spiritual gifts. Therefore, since each and every healing is a gift of the Spirit, it is listed in the plural form.

Avenues of healing

There are several different avenues through which we can receive healing. First, there is preventive healing, which is perhaps the best of all. As we learn to take care of our bodies—eating properly and getting the rest and exercise we need—we will live in health. A second avenue for healing is that which comes through medical science. We do not discount the wisdom that has been unlocked through medical research and study to bring healing to many.

The healing that supersedes these natural means is that which comes through the gifts of healing. Sometimes it is an instantaneous healing in which God does what doctors could not do. At other times it is a progressive healing, as suggested in the Scriptures when we read, "And as they went, they were cleansed" (Luke 17:14). The Scriptures refer also to healing that comes through the Word alone. "He sent His word and healed them and delivered them from their destruction" (Ps. 107:20).

Of course, the age-old question of many is, "Why do some people get healed and others do not?" A dear saintly minister, Brother Ralph Byrd, who has spoken much wisdom into my life, said this to me early in my walk in the Spirit: "God heals enough people to let you know He can, and doesn't heal enough others to let you know that you can't." God has the right to use people as He desires in the area of healing. And, of course, we cannot deny the sovereignty of God in healing as in all other areas of life.

I believe the fact that not everyone is healed ultimately works for our good. It discourages spiritual pride and convinces us of the interdependency on members of the body of Christ. Believers need to recognize that Jesus's healing ministry has been entrusted to the entire body of Christ, not to a few prominent ministers with extraordinary healing gifts. Some believers are frequently used to minister healing, and may be considered to have gifts of healings (1 Cor. 12:30). Yet the Holy Spirit may choose to manifest a gift of healing to any believer who is yielded to Him to meet a specific need. We must always remember that the Healer is Jesus. Healing gifts, however they are manifested, are a direct result of our heavenly Father's enduring love, mercy, and provision for His children.

Although we may continue to grapple with the difficult question of why everyone is not healed of every sickness, we can only respond with heartfelt gratitude each time someone is made whole. No matter how often I have been used to minister healing through the years, I have always seen it as an expression of Jesus's deep compassion for the sick and suffering. Each time someone is healed, I am awed by God's choice to use men and women as His vehicle to deliver His mercy through gifts of healings.

As with the other gifts, we must never forget that what is done must be done by Jesus. We cannot do it. We are not the healer; Jesus heals. He uses human instrumentality, but it is Christ who does the healing. And we must learn to trust our heavenly Father's sovereign wisdom, His time element, and His grace. I believe we are going to see the greatest era of healing we have ever seen in the next move of God.

GIFT OF WORKING OF MIRACLES

To another the working of miracles…

—1 CORINTHIANS 12:10

"The working of miracles" is the translation of the Greek, which literally rendered means "operations of supernatural powers." As with the gifts of healing *energemata dunameon*, these terms are plural. The Scriptures seem to indicate that each miraculous manifestation of power operates along with the gift of faith (Matt. 17:20). In the New Testament events of supernatural origin are called "signs," "wonders," and "miracles" (Acts 2:22, 43; 6:8; Heb. 2:4). They refer to events of divine power that cause wonderment and at the same time reveal something about God's ways. Simply stated, *a miracle is an event or action that seemingly contradicts known scientific laws, superseding them due to a supernatural act of God.*

The miracles of our Lord always bring a revelation of the Father and are signs of His kingdom. They are fingerprints of God's wisdom, love, and mercy. Jesus never acted out of character, so every miracle was in harmony with the revelation of God in Christ. It is noteworthy that the term *wonder* is never used by itself in the Scriptures, but is always found with the term *signs*. For example, we read this: "God also bore them witness with signs and wonders and diverse miracles and with gifts of the Holy Spirit distributed according to His own will" (Heb. 2:4). God does not manifest His power just to cause wonderment alone. He always signifies or teaches something with His signs and miracles that will help in building His kingdom.

Miracles are never pointless spectacles to make people gape; they are life-changing acts of God, reflecting the mind and heart of God that desires to help people. The vast majority of New Testament miracles involved bringing wholeness to peoples' bodies and lives, restoring the blind and lame, casting out demons, and even raising the dead in a moment's time. The gift of miracles, or working of powers, operates immediately in the realm of meeting the needs of men and women.

We should note that there were some miracles in the ministry of Jesus that seem to have accompanied His ministry alone. As we read the Gospels, we see Jesus turning water into wine, stilling storms on the sea, multiplying food, and walking on water. These were performed with the "ultra" motive of revealing His Father to mankind. We do not have any records of His disciples doing these things in their ministries. Paul, for example, did many miracles of healing and deliverance, but he did not still the storms that left him shipwrecked three times.

God can and does sometimes perform miracles in the realm of nature today. However, it is His miracles to people of healing, restoration, and deliverance that are in more abundant evidence. The greatest miracle God is performing today is the redeeming and restoring of mankind in the building of His church. All God's power is miracle power, and Christianity is a miracle movement from start to finish.

The *dunameis* power that the disciples received at Pentecost was a "potency," or latent force waiting to be drawn upon. When the need arose and they responded in faith, this *dunamos* potential exploded into energy. It can be compared to the electrical energy resident in a bulldozer's battery. Faith is like turning the key in the ignition and expecting the power in that battery to loose its electrical energy which surges into the starter and propels the engine. In the early church, as the apostles were obedient to God's calling, many signs and wonders were done through them (Acts 2:43). Soon after Pentecost, for example, Peter and John healed a lame man at the temple gate (Acts 3:1–8). Other examples of miracles in the Scriptures include supernatural deliverance from imprisonment (Acts 5:18–20; 16:23–30); raising the dead (Acts 9:36–42); and Paul shaking off the poisonous viper (Acts 28:3–5).

Healing the sick and casting out demon spirits also may be classified as gifts of miracles when there is a great sign value, as when Paul was at Ephesus and great soul-winning resulted (Acts 19:11). The same is true of Peter when just his shadow's falling upon the sick brought healing (Acts 5:12–15). This sphere of miraculous ministry continued beyond the twelve apostles to Stephen, Philip, and Barnabas, and continued throughout the early church. Although those who work miracles may not have asked specifically for the gift, miracle power is automatically a result of the "package deal" of the Great Commission and Pentecost. Those who obeyed what Jesus commanded found that Jesus would do what He promised.

God often works His miracles through the most unlikely people, such as Philip, the table-waiter. The apostles chose Philip as one of seven men assigned to distribute food to the Greek widows (Acts 6:1–5). The Bible says he was of good reputation and full of the Holy Spirit, which are wonderful qualifications for waiting tables. But Philip discovered his greater potential as he worked diligently to serve God. After the church in Jerusalem was scattered, Philip went to Samaria to preach Christ. There the Lord worked miracles through Philip, and unclean spirits crying with a loud voice came out of many who were possessed (Acts 8).

I believe Philip is a good illustration of the person God uses to work miracles. He was a *faithful worker, a zealous witness, diligent and faithful over a few things*. He worked diligently to preach the good news, and God empowered him through the anointing of the Holy Spirit to work miracles. Unless we obey and go where there is a work to do, the gifts of the Spirit are superfluous. We must make ourselves available to relationship with God first, then to the work of God, and the gifts will come as divine enablements to do that work. They are not for armchair Christians who are not involved in the work of God. Someone has said there is no such thing as an "anointed couch potato."

The key to miracle power

To experience the miracle-working power of God, we must listen to and obey by faith the voice of the Holy Spirit. This is why it has been such a cry of my heart that the church learn to have a personal, intimate relationship with the Holy Spirit. Without that relationship, we will not be able to hear and obey Him. This principle is clearly seen in a memorable miracle of the Gospels, that of Peter walking on the water (Matt. 14:22–33). Peter was exactly where Jesus had commanded him to be: in the boat. From that place of obedience he could step out into the sea, the "miracle area" where Jesus was, but even then only when commanded by Christ. Note that he did not attempt to move until Jesus said, "Come." Peter's faith rested wholly on the word of Christ's command. Although many criticize Peter for taking his eyes off Jesus and sinking, it is only fair to acknowledge that he did walk on water at Jesus's beckoning, which none of us have done.

Again, let us conclude with a word of caution. Presumption is not faith. God is not obligated to do the miracle we ask if we are "showing off," calling attention to ourselves, or enjoying an ego trip. We must patiently wait for God's moment. As we enter the area where a miracle is needed, we should pray, "Lord, what is the key to Your power and anointing for this situation?"

Of course, Jesus offers us the best example of miracle-working. He was found among the poor and beggars, the wretched, the lepers. He lavished love upon the unloved; He healed for no other reason than to reveal the Father's love and His compassion for lost mankind.

To summarize, then, the people who will receive God's gift of miracles are those who: (a) are faithful to any task God has called them; (b) are filled with zeal for the gospel; (c) are servants in situations where the miraculous is needed to do His work; (d) are willing to obey His leading; and (e) are filled with compassion for the hurting. God's manifold purpose for working miracles is to reveal the glory of God, to demonstrate His power and love, to minister to people who know nothing of Jesus, to destroy the works of the enemy, and to terrorize Satan. When we see miracles happening that result in changed lives, deliverance, and healing, we know that Jesus is there. That was the way He ministered when He was on earth, and it is the way He ministers now by His Holy Spirit through His church. Even as Jesus cannot change, but is the same yesterday, today, and forever (Heb. 13:8), so the gift of the working of miracles will remain in the church until His return.

TONGUES AND INTERPRETATION OF TONGUES

> ...to another divers kinds of tongues; to another the interpretation of tongues...
>
> —1 CORINTHIANS 12:10, KJV

In our study of the baptism of the Holy Spirit (chapter 2) we defined and discussed two kinds of tongues that are given to the believer. The tongue of ecstasy accompanies our initial baptism in the Holy Spirit and gives us a wonderful prayer language through which we are personally edified (1 Cor. 14:4). It does not require interpretation, for we are speaking to God, not to men.

The second kind of tongues, described in the Scriptures as "divers kinds of tongues," is given for the edification of the church. It must be interpreted so the message can be understood by all. When Paul gives instructions for public services, he tells the Corinthians to avoid confusion by not speaking in tongues without giving interpretation. Although he acknowledges that he speaks in tongues more than all of them together, he emphasizes the importance of the gift of interpretation functioning in a public service so the church may be edified. Some might ask, "Since tongues that are interpreted are equal to prophecy, according to 1 Corinthians 14:5, why not be content with prophecy?" The Scriptures teach that tongues are a sign for the unbeliever (1 Cor. 14:22). God has ordained tongues to do a work in hearts, and we should give them their rightful place.

As speaking in tongues is not conceived in the mind but comes miraculously by the Spirit of God, so interpretation of tongues emanates from the Spirit rather than from the intellect of man. There is a peculiarity in the gift of tongues, in that it has no meaning without the interpretation. *Interpretation of tongues is the supernatural showing forth by the Spirit of the meaning of an utterance in other tongues.* The interpreter does not understand the tongue he is interpreting; therefore, he is not translating the unknown language. The interpreter simply looks to God in dependence on Him to show forth the meaning just as the speaker in tongues yields in dependence on God for the supernatural utterance. (Although education, temperament, nationality, and similar factors influence our speech patterns, the Lord doesn't choose His mouthpieces because of their fluency in language or even their spiritual maturity. Amos, the farmer, was a prophet of God as well as Isaiah and Jeremiah, who had different cultural backgrounds.) In the mind of God the message in tongues and the interpretation of it are the exact and most blessed link. In the mind of man the two utterances are quite independent, though equally direct from God, requiring dependence on the Holy Spirit for both manifestations.

Purpose for interpretation of tongues

The gift of interpretation makes clear to the understanding of the possessor what has already been an edification of his spirit in other tongues (1 Cor. 14:13–14). Obviously it is not necessary that everything we utter in other tongues in private be given interpretation. But in circumstances where interpretation is necessary or desirable, God will give one so our minds as well as our spirits may profit. Donald Gee, the great Pentecostal theologian, writes:

> The purpose of the gift of interpretation is to render the inspired utterances by the Spirit which have gone forth in a tongue unknown to the vast majority present available to the general understanding of all by repeating them distinctly in the ordinary language of the people assembled. The same Holy Spirit Who inspired the speaking in other tongues whereby the words expressed flow from the Spirit rather than through the intellect is able to inspire the interpretation also. Interpretation is therefore inspirational, ecstatic, spontaneous as the utterance.[2]

Those who speak in other tongues are expressly instructed to pray for the ability to interpret (1 Cor. 14:13). The purpose of this regulation is not to silence those who speak with tongues, but to ensure that the church be edified if no other interpreter is present. It is a safeguard to the church to ensure that there will not be a tongue without an interpretation. One who speaks forth in a tongue in a public service must take the responsibility to interpret if someone else does not. It is significant that although the gift of interpretation of tongues is not distributed exclusively among those who have the gift of tongues, those who speak with tongues are by far the most common possessors of this gift.

The Greek word for *interpretation* in the Corinthian letter means to explain thoroughly, not to translate. This explains why sometimes an utterance in tongues is much longer or shorter than the subsequent interpretation. However, the interpretation can be a literal translation of the message in tongues if the Spirit chooses to give it in that way. Frequently someone in the audience understands the tongue that has been spoken, and God gives a literal translation for the sake of that person's faith. That is what the Holy Spirit did for me. Although I was a minister, I was an "unbeliever" regarding tongues. I heard a message in tongues given in the Hebrew language. Because I had studied some Hebrew and understood part of the interpretation, I was convinced that these gifts were truly a manifestation of the Spirit of God.

The Bible enjoins us to let one interpret. "If any of you use the gift of tongues, not more than two, or three at the most should do so—each speaking in his turn and someone should interpret. If there is no one able to interpret what is said, they should remain silent at the meeting of the church..." (1 Cor. 14:27–28, *20th Century Translation*). This does not mean that the same individual must always interpret in all meetings, nor even that the same person must interpret all messages. "Let one interpret" means that when there is speaking in tongues in a message form, someone must interpret. Moffatt's translation reads as "Let someone interpret." This word further indicates that one individual message should not receive more than one interpretation, even though a dozen worshippers might have been able to interpret it.

A principle in the operation of the gifts is this: the greater the gift, the more faith it takes to operate it. More faith is needed to interpret tongues than to give a message in tongues since it is understood by the human mind. As we learn to yield to the Holy Spirit to allow His gifts to flow through us, our faith will become stronger. In this way the Holy Spirit can use us more effectively to bless the body of Christ.[3]

The third spiritual gift in this group of vocal utterance gifts is, of course, prophecy. Because of the present-day significance that is being given to the restoration of prophecy to the church, I have dedicated the next chapter to a study of prophecy. For that reason we will not define it here. However, before we proceed, we need to mention that the work of the Holy Spirit is not limited to these nine manifestations. There are more than these nine gifts listed in the Scriptures.

Varieties of Gifts

> God has put these in the church: first apostles, second prophets, third teachers, after that miracles, then gifts of healings, helps, governments, and various tongues.
> —1 Corinthians 12:28

Paul is mentioning gifts that were already well known to the Corinthians who came behind in no good gift. How can we express the value of one who functions in the gift of helps when what is needed most is *help?* Yet I have heard those who have this spiritual gift demean themselves by saying, "I just have the gift of helps." We need to evaluate spiritual gifts by how they bless the body of Christ rather than how much recognition they give a person.

To the Romans Paul introduces other gifts that illustrate his purpose of discussion:

> We have diverse gifts according to the grace that is given to us: if prophecy, according to the proportion of faith; if service, in serving; he who teaches, in teaching; he who exhorts, in exhortation; he who gives, with generosity; he who rules, with diligence; he who shows mercy, with cheerfulness.
> —ROMANS 12:6–8

These gifts are ministries given by God as well for the building of the local church. How many have considered *giving* to be a spiritual gift? We need those who exercise this gift as much as those who prophesy. And when mercy is needed, how welcome is the kindness that is received!

Then to the Ephesians Paul wrote concerning five gifts given to the church of Christ:

> He gave some to be apostles, prophets, evangelists, pastors, and teachers, for the equipping of the saints, for the work of service, and for the building up of the body of Christ.
> —EPHESIANS 4:11–12

These gifts given to the church by Christ are different from the gifts given to the church by the Holy Spirit. The spiritual gifts given by the Holy Spirit are resident in the local church to be manifest by the will of the Spirit. The Holy Spirit operates these gifts through believers to edify that local church. In contrast, the gifts Christ gave the church can transcend the local church, becoming a blessing to the whole body of Christ. We call these gifts the five apostolic gifts or the fivefold ministry. These gifts are people, given to the body of Christ and anointed to minister in certain spiritual offices to believers to equip them for the work of the ministry. When God sets apart a person for a spiritual office, He bestows upon him a divine enablement that corresponds to that office, equipping him to do the ministry He has ordained.

Some theologians have limited the number of spiritual gifts to nine to correspond to the nine fruit of the Spirit listed in Galatians 5. But a careful searching of the Scriptures reveals other fruit of the Spirit besides the nine that are listed there. For example, Peter admonishes Christians:

> …make every effort to add virtue to your faith; and to your virtue, knowledge; and to your knowledge, self-control; and to your self-control, patient endurance; and to your patient endurance, godliness; and to your godliness, brotherly kindness; and to your brotherly kindness, love.
>
> —2 Peter 1:5–7

Paul also mentions seventeen works of the flesh and ends the list with the phrase "and such like." Surely if the flesh can produce more than seventeen evil works, the Holy Spirit can produce a greater number of virtues that reveal an aspect of divine love. Failing to recognize all the gifts that God has given to the church will only limit our capacity for receiving the blessings that He intends for us to enjoy.

Summary

The Holy Spirit stood with Peter and filled him, not only on the Day of Pentecost, but also when he stood before the Sanhedrin and testified boldly that there was no other name under heaven whereby men could be saved (Acts 4:8–12). In the Book of Acts (which could be called the Acts of the Holy Spirit) the Holy Spirit dominated the scene. Through Peter and John, Stephen, Philip, Paul, Barnabas, Silas, Agabus, and others, the Holy Spirit was the invisible, divine Comforter who had taken Christ's place as teacher and leader among His disciples. At the Council in Jerusalem, at the church in Antioch, and all similar deliberations, He administered the affairs of the church. Through the gifts of government, from the original visitation in the parent church at Jerusalem to similar visitations in the churches at Samaria, Cesarea, Antioch, Pisidia, Galatia, Ephesus, and Corinth, the Holy Spirit personally filled the believers. What Christ could not do when He walked on the earth as a man, the Holy Spirit did by indwelling the lives of these yielded believers and working through them the mighty works and words of power like those that were wrought in Jesus's ministry.

This very real commander in chief led His infant church on to victory. That was the secret of the phenomenal success of the early church. They were unlearned men, without silver or gold. Their church machinery was very simple, made up of prophets, evangelists, pastors, teachers, elders, and deacons. They were men and women who were bound together chiefly by ties of love and a common purpose. They had no prestige. Paul declared that the apostles were made as the filth of the world, an off-scouring of all things (1 Cor. 4:13). They were the sect that was everywhere spoken against, yet they turned the world upside down. The gospel was preached to every creature under heaven, and churches were established. The only explanation for this phenomenal success was the fact that the apostles and their converts were filled with the Holy Spirit. The Holy Spirit was honored and given proper authority and control over their lives. He indwelt believers with power, investing them with His gifts. He went with them to prison, to the martyr's stake, to the whipping post. They went with Him, and He with them. Together, the Holy Spirit and His body, the body of Christ, marched on to amazing victory, through the apostolic days.

May we be admonished that this is the need of the church today. The prophet declared:

> And it will be that, afterwards, I will pour out My Spirit on all flesh; then your sons and your daughters will prophesy, your old men will dream dreams, and your young men will see visions. Even on the menservants and maidservants in those days I will pour out My Spirit.
>
> —JOEL 2:28–29

Truly the need of the church in this hour is for the Holy Spirit to be given His rightful place of authority and honor so the gifts of the Spirit can flow in purity and power. Paul exhorted the Thessalonians to "not quench the Spirit" (1 Thess. 5:19). May we not be guilty of quenching the Spirit in our assemblies today, but follow Paul's exhortation to give the Holy Spirit His liberty to move among us. Only in that way can He reveal to us the things of Jesus and be allowed to build His church effectively in the earth.

Chapter 5

Gifts of the Holy Spirit

Part III:
Divine Voice-Prophecy

. . . .

For the testimony of Jesus is the spirit of prophecy.

—REVELATION 19:10

. . . .

ECAUSE OF THE impact prophecy is making on the church today, both negatively and positively, I feel there is a need to understand clearly what the Scriptures teach concerning prophecy, the prophet, the gift of prophecy, and the spirit of prophecy. The present emphasis on the prophetic ministry in the church has brought great blessing where it has been properly understood. It has also brought devastation to individual lives and churches when scriptural guidelines have not been followed for its operation. God's Word clearly teaches the parameters of true prophecy in all its dimensions. Only as we apply ourselves diligently to obey these principles will we benefit from God-given prophecy and be protected from what is false.

There is a desire in all of us to know the future—economically, politically, and especially spiritually. I once heard that the psychics' telephone number announced on television was the most-called number ever made available on television. Although we condemn psychic power because of its ungodly source, I mention it to show how badly people want someone to tell them what is going to happen.

To have a prophetic anointing from the Holy Spirit to declare truth is not the same as giving an educated prediction. It is more than divine inspiration or even revelation at times. Prophecy is more than one of the nine gifts listed in 1 Corinthians. True prophecy is *a divine ability to accurately perceive and proclaim present spiritual realities and to predict and prepare for the future.* One writer has referred to prophecy as the early winds of the coming season blowing across the earth. It is the dawn of tomorrow coming through the night of a dying day.

When the church truly functions as God intended, it functions *prophetically.* Because the Scriptures declare that the testimony of Jesus is the spirit of prophecy, we understand that if our Lord's voice is being heard in the church speaking through Spirit-filled believers, we are hearing a voice of prophecy. He will speak through such vehicles as (a) prophetic preaching; (b) the office of the prophet; (c) the gift of prophecy; (d) musical prophecies; (e) the song of the Lord and of the bride to the Bridegroom; (f) prophetic prayers; and even (g) the prophetic reading of the Scriptures.

Prophecy demonstrated in the Scriptures

As we have stated, true prophecy is the divine ability to perceive, predict, proclaim, and prepare for the future. Prophecy in the Old Testament is depicted as both human activity and divine activity. God is the source of the prophetic message, and human vessels become the channel for relating that message to the people concerned. Two Old Testament Hebrew words depict these divine and human aspects of prophecy. The Hebrew word *nataf* means "to fall as drops of rain." This word pictures the divine activity of prophecy as the prophetic message proceeds from God, falling from heaven like raindrops. *Naba* is the Hebrew word for prophecy that means "to bubble up or gush forth." This word shows the human activity involved in prophecy, our human response to the prophetic anointing of God. The prophetic message pours forth from the prophet as water bubbling and gushing from a fountain.

A prophetic utterance is also described in Scripture as "the word of the Lord," from the Hebrew word *dabar*. The etymological meaning of this word is "to drive forward that which is behind." Thus the prophetic word has a creative force that drives forward to accomplish its message. This concept of a prophetic word having a dynamic creative force is also described by Paul in the New Testament. He requested the church in Thessalonica to pray for them that the word of the Lord would have free course (2 Thess. 3:1). The Greek word *trecho*, which is translated to "have free course," literally means "to run." This word is descriptive of a Greek runner who is running a course on which there are no barriers or hindrances to impede his progress. Thus Paul is asking for prayer that there will be nothing to impede the creative force of the word of the Lord from running—driving forward to its accomplishment.

In the New Testament, prophecy is further defined by the Greek word *propheteuo*, a declaration from God that could include prediction of the future as well as proclamation of divine realities. Prophecy has a foretelling, predictive aspect as a human vessel speaks for God concerning a future situation of the people. It may also be simply forthtelling in a proclamative aspect as a human vessel becomes God's mouthpiece to speak to the present situation of the people.

In summary we can say that prophecy is a supernatural utterance by which God communicates to people His mind and purpose, using a Spirit-filled individual as His mouthpiece. Prophecy as *foretelling* involves prediction. In this realm the prophet speaks for God, communicating what he perceives to be God's mind for the future. Past and present can be used to deal with the future. The purpose of prophetic prediction is to produce present godliness and edification in light of the future. Prophecy as *forthtelling* is proclamation, often involving anointed preaching. Sometimes the prophet will use the past to explain the present. This realm includes exhortation, reproof, warning, comfort, and edification. The prophet is a "preacher" and "proclaimer" of the Word of the Lord. True prophecy, then, will contain one or both of these messages: prediction of future events and present instruction concerning God's will.

Purpose of prophecy

Since the Scriptures teach that "the testimony of Jesus is the spirit of prophecy" (Rev. 19:10), we understand that the purpose of prophecy is first of all the exaltation of Jesus. The Holy Spirit came to glorify Jesus (John 16:14), and the Father has highly exalted Him above every name in heaven and earth (Phil. 2:9). As the head of the church, Christ must receive honor in every manifestation of the Spirit of God. Therefore, prophecy that exalts a person or group of people is immediately suspect because the primary purpose for the coming of the Holy Spirit is to reveal Jesus.

Second, prophecy is a means of receiving verbal communication from God in our known languages. Paul said that one who speaks in tongues speaks mysteries unto God; no one understands him. But the one who prophesies speaks unto men (1 Cor. 14:2–3). In that sense prophecy gives vocal expression to other spiritual gifts as well. For example, gifts of knowledge need the prophetic anointing for their expression to the body of Christ. Even gifts of power often need the gift of prophecy for articulation of their manifestations.

Third, prophecy is meant to bring edification to the church (v. 4). Prophecy should build up, not tear down; it should comfort, not condemn; it should instruct, not injure. God has given us the prophetic voice in all of its manifestations to exalt Jesus and to bless and build the church. What a wonder it is that God would speak to mankind through a human vessel! How careful we should be to guard the integrity of His voice.

It is an awesome responsibility to minister under a prophetic anointing given by the Holy Spirit. For a prophet to rightly predict a future event or trend gives him or her great authority with people. For this reason, care must be taken not to use the true prophetic anointing to manipulate people to follow a person's ministry. If a person has to wear a badge or make an announcement declaring that he or she is a prophet, that one is not a prophet.

At times the Holy Spirit will speak a word of correction to a church through the prophetic word. It is important to note, however, that the ministry of *corrective prophecy* belongs only to the leader of the flock or to another minister properly submitted to that pastoral leadership. A lay person should never attempt to correct, condemn, or chastise a congregation or an individual through the use of the gift of prophecy. According to the Scriptures the simple gift of prophecy that operates apart from the office of a prophet is to be used for edification, comfort, and exhortation (v. 3). Correction of a church or believer corresponds to the office of the prophet, to one who is walking in a place of responsibility and accountability before

God for a particular group of people. The purpose of prophecy, then, is first to exalt Jesus and then to build the body of Christ.

Prophets and apostles

To understand the restoration of the prophetic ministry to the church, we must examine the biblical relationship between apostles and prophets. According to the Scriptures the revelation of the great mystery of Christ regarding the church was given to the apostles and prophets (Eph. 3:2–6). Paul teaches that the church is built on the foundation laid by the apostles and prophets (1 Cor. 3:9–15; Eph. 2:19–22). All other ministries are to be built upon this foundation. In divine order, though all are equal in value as persons before the Lord, God has set some in the church to be apostles, prophets, evangelists, teachers, and pastors, for the equipping of the saints (Eph. 4:11). These are different and unique gifts that in the wisdom of God are sent to the body of Christ.

The Scriptures teach, by example, that the apostle and prophet are called to work together, to act as checks and balances for one another. I think it is dangerous for an apostle or a prophet to work alone, at least without conferring with one another and sharing their ministry together. We need to hear as a unit what the Spirit is saying to the church. It is also clear from the Scriptures that apostles function in a governmental capacity in the church, while prophets function in a revelatory capacity. Although we would not rule out the possibility of one person functioning under both anointings, we recognize the safety of having both apostles and prophets working together in the church. We must beware lest we exalt one over the other. As we begin to understand the need for prophecy in the building of the church, we realize how important it is for the apostles and the prophets to work together in a proper relationship.

Prophets are given by Christ, the head of His body, to perfect that body through revelation. They are viewed as messengers, seers, communicators, and encouragers of the church. Their mission is to communicate what the Holy Spirit has confirmed to the apostolic leadership and to edify the local churches. Prophets are not intended to set up personal dynasties and to make the other giftings inferior to the office of prophecy.

New Testament examples of prophets such as Silas and Judas (Acts 15:32) and Agabus (Acts 21:10) were men who were recognized "trans-locally" as those whose prophetic ministry strengthened the local churches. It was Agabus, a prophet gifted as a seer of future events, who prophesied the apostle Paul's imprisonment (v. 11). Before his conversion Paul was a dedicated Pharisee who desperately resisted the emerging church. But after his conversion he was given prophetic insight into the coming season of the church. Jesus appeared to him, and he saw a light brighter than the midday sun, brighter than Phariseeism, Judaism, and all other lights. That new light that began to illumine his life brought revelation of Christ and His kingdom.

Not only was the apostle Paul personally transformed, but also the eternal plan of God for the church that was revealed through him changed the world. He saw the startling mystery that had been hidden in God since before the foundation of the world until that time. He saw that God was going to bring all people together in Christ according to His eternal plan. He saw that the old boundaries were obliterated at the cross. He realized that this revelation was contrary to all he had believed before. And when he saw it, he moved from merely being religious to becoming prophetic, as well as apostolic. Paul not only proclaimed the change he saw, but as an apostle born out of due season, he also helped to make it happen by establishing churches through the power of the Holy Spirit.

Today prophets and prophetesses are divinely given ministries to help build strong churches during this transitional period. The churches that are moving on the cutting edge of what God is doing today, hearing what God by His Spirit is saying, are those that are allowing the prophetic ministry to be restored to them. We have seen this restoration of the true prophetic ministry throughout the last several decades by the correct emphasis being placed on prophetic insight in the church.

As with each movement of the Holy Spirit, however, there have been extremes, as well as overemphases of the truth. It is said that he who walks the razor edge of truth also walks the razor edge of heresy. This has seemed particularly true concerning the prophetic ministry. Although this God-ordained ministry has been abused, misused, and mis-taught, it is still the ministry Jesus set in the church; it has not passed away. There will always be those who respond to truth in faith, and others who will respond in fear through unbelief. We need to place our faith in God and accept the ministry of the prophetic in the fear of God as it is properly restored to the church.

For the restoration of the prophetic ministry to be effective in the church, it is important to understand the nature of prophecy as well as some biblical parameters given for the proper discerning of the prophetic voice. This will keep us from erroneous teaching regarding prophecy and will prevent us from making everyone a "prophet." Man-made prophets are not set in the church by Christ. In order for the church to prosper, we need the true ministry of the prophet to function as Christ intended.

THE CHAIN OF PROPHECY

The Prophecy of Scripture

> We have also a reliable sure word of prophecy....For no prophecy at any time was produced by the will of man, but holy men moved by the Holy Spirit spoke from God.
> —2 PETER 1:19, 21, KJV

Because the Scriptures are the inspired, infallible words of God, the prophecy of Scripture is regarded as infallible revelation (2 Tim. 3:16). This kind of prophecy is not being spoken today because the sixty-six books of the Bible, the canon of Scripture, are complete. According to the Scriptures nothing is to be added or taken away from the Word of God (Rev. 22:18–19). Prophecy of Scripture refers to all the Scriptures generally, and more specifically to the prophetic books of the Old Testament. This is the highest level of prophecy, deserving our complete confidence and requiring the most careful and systematic interpretation.

Of course, this level of prophecy is not subject to judging; it is infallible and is the basis for judging all other realms of prophecy. Although we do not judge the utterance of the Scriptures, the Scriptures do judge our utterances, whatever they are. There is no present truth of greater authority than the Word of God, and no one whose prophecy is above being judged for its validity by the Word of God.

The office of the prophet

> God, who at various times and in diverse ways spoke
> long ago to the fathers through the prophets.
>
> —HEBREWS 1:1

In Old Testament times a prophet was a person given to the distinctive ministry of representing God before mankind through a prophetic mantle that came upon him. The prophet was God's mouthpiece, God's spokesman, through whom the Word of God flowed, whether in forthtelling or foretelling. God established the office of the prophet for the people of Israel, who asked not to hear the voice of the Lord for themselves (Deut. 18:15–19). Such men as Samuel, Elijah, and Amos filled the office of prophet. Women such as Deborah (Judg. 4:4), Huldah (2 Chron. 34:22), and Anna (Luke 2:36–38), were prophetesses. A true prophet or prophetess becomes a representative of God to the people. We have already mentioned New Testament prophets who were gifts to the church to build it through revelation received from God.

The gift of prophecy

> We have diverse gifts according to the grace that is given
> to us: if prophecy, according to the proportion of faith.
>
> —ROMANS 12:6

The gift of prophecy as listed with the other nine gifts of the Spirit (1 Cor. 12:8–10), is defined as the God-given ability to speak forth supernaturally in a known language as the Holy Spirit gives utterance. The meanings of the Hebrew and Greek words describing this gift involve ecstatic vision, burden, and inspired utterances, and can be translated as, "to break forth under sudden impulse in lofty discourse on praise or the divine counsels." This is an operation of the Holy Spirit as seen in the New Testament church that must be exercised within divine guidelines. It is not infallible.

As we have stated, the gift of prophecy functions in three areas: edification, which means *building up*; exhortation, which is *stirring up*; and comfort, which could be called *cheering up*. Paul taught, "But he who prophesies speaks to men for their edification and exhortation and comfort" (1 Cor. 14:3). These are safe guidelines that everyone who prophesies can follow.

It is important that we approach each of the gifts in an attitude of humility. If someone gives an utterance that is not received by those who are discerning and judging by the Spirit, the one giving the utterance should not be offended. In a teachable spirit that person should receive the correction given and pray to become more sensitive to the Holy Spirit. As believers we should not become discouraged with the imperfectness in prophetic utterances. Rather we need to heed the admonition of Paul when he says, "Do not quench the Spirit. Do not despise prophecies. Examine all things. Firmly hold onto what is good" (1 Thess. 5:19–21). Heeding this scriptural teaching on spiritual gifts will prevent immature and misguided manifestations that become a temptation to some to quench the moving of the Spirit.

The Office and Gift Contrasted

Having defined the office of the prophet and the gift of prophecy, perhaps a further contrasting of their functions will give greater clarity to their uniqueness. The office and the gift are distinct for two reasons:

1. According to the Scriptures the office of the prophet is inseparable from the person: "And He gave some as apostles, and some as prophets..." (Eph. 4:11, NAS). The prophet is one of the five-fold ministries Christ gave to the church. The person who functions in the office of a prophet has a prophetic mantle continually resting upon him or her. The gift of prophecy, on the contrary, is one of the nine gifts Paul lists (1 Cor. 12:8–10), for which the Holy Spirit can use anyone in the church who is yielded to Him when He chooses to speak prophetically at a certain time.

2. Far greater gifts than this simple gift of prophecy are needed to make a man a prophet. For example, revelation of hidden things of the past, present, or future are necessary for the prophetic office. Nathan the prophet, who exposed King David's sin with Bathsheba, is an example (2 Sam. 12). This type of revelation is not included in the realm of the gift of prophecy.

Exercising the gift of prophecy, then, does not necessarily result in a person becoming a prophet. Paul's exhortation to seek to prophesy does not relate to the office of the prophet, but to the gift of prophecy (1 Cor. 14:1). So it is possible to operate the gift of prophecy and not be fulfilling the office of a prophet. It is not possible, however, to be a prophet without having the gift of prophecy. Simply stated, *all prophets will prophesy, but all who prophesy are not prophets.* The gift of prophecy comes well down the list in order of importance among the gifts, but the prophetic office is second among the offices (Eph. 4:11).

We would use these words to describe the office of prophet: representative of God, permanent office, lifestyle, greater authority. In contrast we would describe the gift of prophecy as follows: present expression of God's mind, temporary anointing. The gift of prophecy and the office of the prophet are similar, however, in that they are both subject to judgment by the saints on the basis of the Word, the Spirit, and the blood.

Manifestation of the gift of prophecy

The gift of prophecy will be manifested, first of all, in vocal utterances in public worship services. Peter exhorted:

> If anyone speaks, let him speak as the oracles of God.
> —1 PETER 4:11

The Greek word for oracle is *logion*, which means a short utterance or short word. It can be a part of a longer utterance that includes exhorting and confirming teaching.

Second, the gift of prophecy can bring forth a message to an individual. God will sometimes encourage and edify a person with a word of prophecy. I would hasten to caution those who give or receive a personal word of prophecy, however, for it must be judged like any other prophetic word. The person receiving the prophetic word should submit it to his or her pastoral leadership that is responsible to give an account before God for the souls under their care (Heb. 13:17). I personally have seen many lives hurt and churches split through the improper use of this gift. There is safety in following scriptural guidelines in the function of spiritual gifts.

The spirit of prophecy

> I fell at his feet to worship him. But he said to me, "See that you not do that. I am your fellow servant, and of your brothers who hold the testimony of Jesus. Worship God! For the testimony of Jesus is the spirit of prophecy."
>
> —REVELATION 19:10

The spirit of prophecy is an all-inclusive term that refers to the Holy Spirit energizing men and women, causing them to speak forth inspired utterances in a known language. Since Jesus is the testimony of prophecy, when He is genuinely speaking through the members He has set in the body, the spirit of prophecy is present. When the spirit of prophecy moves upon a church, it seems that everyone can prophesy because of the anointing of the Holy Spirit flowing at that time. On such an occasion, according to the Scriptures, all may prophesy, though it doesn't mean that all have to or should. Paul gave instructions concerning the orderly use of the gifts in the church: "For you may all prophesy one by one, that all may learn and all may be encouraged" (1 Cor. 14:31). During these refreshing times when the spirit of prophecy is flowing in the church, it is easy for people to prophesy who would not otherwise operate freely in that gift.

The Old Testament scriptures are full of examples of the spirit of prophecy coming upon godly men. For example, Adam prophesied concerning his bride and the marriage estate (Gen. 2:20–25). Enoch prophesied of the second coming of Christ (Jude 14–15). Noah was the preacher of righteousness because the spirit of Christ was upon Him (2 Pet. 2:5). Abraham was spoken of as a prophet (Gen. 20:7). Isaac and Jacob had the spirit of prophecy upon them as they blessed their sons (Gen. 27, 48, 49). Joseph prophesied of the exodus from Egypt (Gen.

50:24). At times the spirit of prophecy even came upon groups of people. The Lord took the same spirit that was upon Moses and placed it upon the seventy elders of Israel and they prophesied (Num. 11:24–30). During the reign of Saul, the spirit of prophecy fell upon several groups of messengers as well as upon King Saul (1 Sam. 19:23–24).

In the New Testament, as we have seen, Paul instructed the churches that tongues are for a sign to the unbeliever and that prophecy serves those who believe. He said that if an unbeliever came in and heard the church prophesying, he would be convinced of all: "Thus the secrets of his heart are revealed. And so falling down on his face, he will worship God and report that God is truly among you" (1 Cor. 14:25). The testimony of Jesus in the church will draw men unto Himself.

Under the influence of the spirit of prophecy, sometimes exhortations are received and *written* before the saints gather together. They can then be shared with the saints when they gather. Writing it down preserves its simplicity, its authenticity, and unction. Also, the spirit of prophecy will break forth in times of *prayer* while we are praying publicly. I personally experienced that at the beginning of my walk in the Spirit. I was praying for a person and heard the Holy Spirit changing my prayer and prophesying through it. I didn't know I was prophesying, but others told me what was happening. Then I began to experience the anointing of the prophetic mantle also when I preached the Word.

It is not uncommon for the Holy Spirit to intersperse the operation of the gift of prophecy with the ministry of teaching. It does not come as an interruption of a "thus saith the Lord" but flows into the anointed teaching. Even *reading the Scriptures aloud* can be done under a prophetic anointing. Although Satan quotes the Scriptures like a parrot, the Holy

Spirit proclaims them like a prophet. We need to live in such a way as to experience the spirit of prophecy in our assemblies, that the testimony of Jesus may be given His proper place in the church.

The prophetic in music

How beautifully the Scriptures describe the prophetic anointing in music and worship! The psalmist, David, who provided so many prophetic songs for us, declared that God Himself inhabits our praises (Ps. 22:3). Paul taught the New Testament church to "let the word of Christ dwell in you richly in all wisdom, teaching and admonishing one another in psalms and hymns and spiritual songs, singing with grace in your hearts to the Lord" (Col. 3:16). He declared that he would sing with the spirit as well as with the understanding (1 Cor. 14:15). What we refer to today as the "song of the Lord" was established under the reign of Hezekiah as he restored worship to Israel (2 Chron. 29:25–28). When Jeremiah prophesied of the restoration of Israel, he declared:

> …Again there shall be heard in this place…the voice of gladness, the voice of the bridegroom, and the voice of the bride, the voice of those who shall say, "Give thanks to the Lord of Hosts, for the Lord is good; for His mercy endures forever," and of those who bring the sacrifice of praise into the house of the Lord. For I will restore the fortunes of the land as at the first, says the Lord.
>
> —Jeremiah 33:10–11

We see another example of the prophetic song when Miriam sang of the great deliverance God had given (Exod. 15:20–21). The song of Moses sung by the saints is prophetic

(Rev. 15:3–4). And is not the Song of Songs the prophetic song of the bridegroom to the bride, as well as her response to her bridegroom? In light of these biblical teachings we should expect the prophetic flow of the Holy Spirit to be a part of our corporate worship in our churches today. For the restoration of the prophetic to the church, we need to allow Him to move in our midst, refreshing us and instructing us through prophetic song and instrumental music.

GUIDELINES FOR DISCERNING PROPHECY

Limitations to prophecy

Although the source of prophecy is divine, the human element is never set aside as the prophecy is communicated to man. For that reason the flow of prophecy through us will have certain limitations. According to Paul, one of the main causes of these limitations is our limited knowledge. He declared that "we know in part, and we prophesy in part" (1 Cor. 13:9). Paul also instructed us to "prophecy, according to the proportion of faith" (Rom. 12:6). Our faith level is another limitation for the prophetic flow through us and usually determines its effectiveness as well. If we do not believe it is God speaking through us, no one else is going to believe it. If the message is given in fear, that fear will be transmitted through the message, diluting its impact. Because these human elements will always be present to some degree, the Scriptures give clear guidelines concerning the proper way to discern and judge the prophetic ministry.

Biblical testings

It is important to subject all prophecy to biblical tests, not only because of human limitations, but also because Satan will stir up false prophets to deceive people. God has given us descriptions of and warnings against false prophets, as well as proofs of a real prophet and genuine prophetic gifts. The tests given in the Word of God help us determine the validity of prophetic utterances.

Test of humility (1 Cor. 8:1). The first test to apply to all prophets and prophetic utterances is the test of humility. First Corinthians 8:1 teaches that knowledge puffs up, but charity edifies. Even though supernatural knowledge is present in the prophetic flow, the result should be the edifying of the church or individual through love. We should answer these questions to be sure humility is working in the prophetic ministry: Does the prophetic voice produce pride in our hearts? Does it exalt a person or Christ? Any personal exaltation of the one prophesying or of those to whom the prophecy is directed must be suspect. True prophecy will work in love through humility.

Test of Spirit (1 John 4:1–3). Is it the Holy Spirit, the human spirit, or an evil spirit that is responsible for the utterance? All three of these spirits can enter into the realm of prophecy and each must be discerned by spiritual people.

Test of worship (Deut. 13:1–5). Does the prophetic word lead us to worship God or lead us away from the true God?

Test of covetousness (Mic. 3:11; 2 Pet. 2:1–3). Are these prophets making merchandise of the people of God? Often one of the characteristics of a false prophet is covetousness.

Test of fulfillment (Deut. 18:22). Does the prophetic word come to pass or not? Time is the great prover of prophecies. We must also remember, however, that fulfillment of a prophetic word is not always immediate.

Test of doctrine (Isa. 8:19–20; John 14:1–6; 1 Tim. 4:1–3). Do the prophets speak in harmony with the major doctrines of redemption? Do they speak according to sound doctrine based on God's Word?

Test of fruit (Matt. 7:15–23). What is the fruit of the prophet's lifestyle? The Scriptures teach that by their fruits, not their gifts, we shall know them. Holiness of life will characterize a true prophet.

Test of ministry to people (Jer. 23:18–23). Do these prophets turn the people from their sinful lifestyles to God? Building the church through prophecy will result in a holy people that love God.

Test of value (1 Tim. 1:18). We are to fight the good fight of faith by the prophecies that go before us. Do we value the infallible Word of God above personal prophetic words? Prophetic words instruct on a personal basis what the inspired and infallible Word of God has already told us to do on a general basis. They must never be allowed higher value in our thinking than the Word of God.

Test of confirmation (Col. 3:15). Is the prophetic utterance confirmation to our spirits? Does it agree with the already revealed will of God? Does it agree with the rule of peace in our hearts? If not, we must seek the counsel of proven ministry.

Test of accountability (Matt. 12:34–37). To whom is this prophet accountable? Does the prophet have an apostolic covering? Is the prophet willing to take responsibility for his or her prophecy? All New Testament prophets belonged to and were under the authority of a local church. To the first-century church Paul wrote that two or three prophets should speak, and the others should weigh carefully what was said (1 Cor. 14:29).

Test of control (2 Pet. 2:1–3). According to the Scriptures, false prophets will exploit people out of greed, introducing heresies and leading people astray through their sensuality. Prophets are not to use their gifts to manipulate, intimidate, or control through fear the people to whom they minister out of selfish motives. Do they attempt to exercise control over believers' lives? Do their utterances manipulate or intimidate? If so, they are not true prophets.

Test of love (1 Cor. 14:3; James 3:17). Prophetic messages should be given in a spirit of love. Even a word of correction is to be given in a spirit of love. Information about any visions that may be negative or embarrassing should never be spoken publicly without first confronting the individual in private.

God's call to the prophetic

We should not neglect to evaluate the prophetic flow in these biblical ways so we can keep from being misguided by the human element or deceived by the work of Satan. These principles are God's safeguards for exercising the prophetic ministry in the body of Christ today. Having considered them, though, we would be careful again to say, with Paul, that we should not despise prophesyings. It is our responsibility to prove all things and hold fast to that which is good so the church can be built effectively.

God is calling the church to the prophetic; He is restoring the ministry of prophecy to the church. He has trusted us with divine abilities in the realm of prophecy, and we need to prove ourselves trustworthy vessels of His power. We must allow the Holy Spirit to use prophecy correctly for the building of the church. Let's not miss it by "throwing out the baby with the bath water" just because some abuse it. As we yield our lives to the Holy Spirit to obey in all things, we will become vessels of honor for the fulfillment of His purposes.

Chapter 6

The Fruit of the Spirit

Part I:
Divine Character Defined

. . . .

But the fruit of the Spirit is love, joy, peace, patience, gentleness, goodness, faith [faithfulness], meekness, and self-control; against such there is no law.

—GALATIANS 5:22–23

But now, having been freed from sin and having become slaves of God, you have fruit unto holiness, and the end is eternal life.

—ROMANS 6:22

. . . .

*I*T IS NO accident that the Word calls the third Person of the Godhead the *Holy Spirit*. Holiness characterizes His divine nature. One of the supreme mandates of the Holy Spirit is to impart the holiness of God to us to change us from glory to glory, giving us His divine nature and His character. As He works in each believer, He develops within us His character, which is identified by the fruit of the Spirit. God's purpose in redeeming us is that we become "a mature man, to the

108

measure of the stature which belongs to the fullness of Christ" (Eph. 4:13, NAS).

I used to think the fruit of the Spirit was produced just like the gifts are, by the Holy Spirit. But then I began to realize that it is not the Spirit Himself who bears the fruit, but the Christ-life within us that produces the fruit of godly character in us. The Holy Spirit produces the Christ-life in us as we obey Him, causing the holiness and divine nature of our Lord Jesus to be manifest through us. The fruit of the Spirit, then, is the true character of the Christian life that replaces the self-life, or old man, as the Scriptures label our sin nature. It is the fruit of the Tree of Life, Christ, who lives in the garden of our spirits. Perry Brewster makes this observation regarding fruit-bearing Christians:

> In some ways the term "Christlikeness" is inadequate. Since the Christian is called not really to resemble Christ but to share His very life. With deference to a great Christian classic, the life of the believer is more than the "Imitation of Christ." It is becoming a partaker of the divine nature (II Pet. 1:4). One might be bold enough to suggest that "Christness" would be nearer the mark, since the believer is more than a copy of Christ. He is part and parcel of His very being. "Bone of His bone, flesh of His flesh," as Paul daringly puts it (Eph. 5:30). Our likeness to Christ is definitely not something applied from without, as a cosmetic transformation produced by a formula of some religious make-up department. It is a genuine likeness produced by an intimate relationship with Him. Christ's own analogy of the vine and the branches upholds this (John 15:1). The branches are not merely vinelike; they are a part of the vine.

Likewise the fruit does not merely resemble grapes, but possesses their inherent structure and taste.[1]

Fruitfulness is the principal purpose for the existence of a tree. Jesus taught His disciples that fruitfulness was His purpose for them as well. He told them, "You did not choose Me, but I chose you, and appointed you, that you should go and bear fruit, and that your fruit should remain..." (John 15:16). In this great teaching Jesus called Himself the true vine, and His Father the husbandman. He called the disciples branches and told them to abide in Him so they could bring forth fruit. He warned them, "Every branch in Me that does not bear fruit, He [the Father] takes away; and every branch that bears fruit, He prunes it, that it may bear more fruit" (John 15:2, NAS).

Jesus cursed the fig tree because it did not bring forth fruit, and in the morning the disciples found the tree had died (Matt. 21:18–19). Does He not have the right to expect to find fruit on His tree of life in His garden? Even the Old Testament carries this beautiful analogy of the bride being a fruitful garden that the bridegroom can enjoy. In the most poetic book of all we read this:

> A garden locked is my sister, my bride, a fountain sealed....a garden fountain, a well of living water, and flowing streams from Lebanon. Awake, O north wind, and come, O south wind! Blow upon my garden, that its spices may flow out. Let my beloved come to his garden, and eat its choicest fruits. I come to my garden, my sister, my bride; I gather my myrrh with my spice; I eat my honeycomb with my honey; I drink my wine with my milk. Eat, friends! Drink, and be drunk with love!
> —SONG OF SONGS 4:12, 15–16; 5:1

Thus fruitfulness is a result of a relationship that is carefully cultivated. Jesus taught His disciples they could only be fruitful by learning to abide in Him.

Principle of Abiding

The principle of abiding must be clearly understood so we avoid trying to bear fruit in our own strength. The Scriptures teach that these true Christian virtues are the fruit of the Spirit, not the fruit of human effort. Many people today are attempting to produce the fruit of the Spirit through natural efforts and character-building. They exercise their wills to produce character through philosophy, education, ethics, anthropology, mental sciences, or controlled environment. The results achieved from this human effort, though they may involve temporal good, are not the eternal fruitfulness that is produced by the work of the Holy Spirit.

Fruit is character.

We have stated that the fruit of the Spirit is the character of Christ produced by the Spirit of Christ in the believer's life. The more completely one is filled with the Holy Spirit, the greater will be the manifestation of the fruit of the Spirit in his life and work. Only when a believer is full of the Holy Spirit, continually yielding to Him, can he exhibit the full fruition of Christian virtues. When Christ is formed in the believer through the indwelling of the Holy Spirit, true Christlike character will be as natural a result as pears growing on a pear tree. It follows then that if one who professes to be a Christian is devoid of fruit, he obviously does not have the Spirit of Christ. The fruit of the Spirit is produced automatically when we are yielded to the Holy Spirit and are walking in obedience to Him.

When Paul describes the fruit of the Spirit in writing to the Galatians, he is restating the Sermon on the Mount. This description is the ideal Christian life presented in concentrated expression. Paul's love chapter to the Corinthians (1 Cor. 13) is the summary of his list of the fruit of the Spirit. He is teaching the very same principle of Christian life when he writes to the Philippians: "...whatever is true, whatever is honorable, whatever is right, whatever is pure, whatever is lovely, whatever is of good repute, if there is any excellence and if anything worthy of praise, dwell on these things" (Phil. 4:8, NAS). Any concept of Christianity that does not have as its basis the character of the fruit of the Spirit is a false teaching of Christianity.

The Scriptures clearly teach that natural man cannot hope to develop godly character without the work of the Holy Spirit in his life. Paul describes the striking contrast between the works of the flesh and the fruit of the Spirit:

> Now the deeds of the flesh are evident, which are: immorality, impurity, sensuality, idolatry, sorcery, enmities, strife, jealousy, outbursts of anger, disputes, dissensions, factions, envying, drunkenness, carousing, and things like these, of which I forewarn you just as I have forewarned you, that those who practice such things shall not inherit the kingdom of God.
>
> —GALATIANS 5:19–21, NAS

Spirit-filled men and women can be distinguished by their fruit in the same way that a carnal person can be identified by fleshly works. If we are abiding in Christ, the fruit of the Spirit will be manifest in our lives; it cannot be hidden. So, also, are the works of the flesh manifest in one who is not abiding in

Christ. A carnal person is one who is not governed by the indwelling Spirit of God. This egocentric, self-centered life manifests the works of the flesh, while a Christ-centered life will manifest the fruit of the Spirit.

The great struggle within each believer is the struggle between self and Christ. If self wins, it becomes the central force of life, causing a person to be completely self-centered. Every descriptive characteristic of a self-centered person starts with the word *self*: selfish, self-pitying, self-glorying, perhaps even self-hating. The list of "self" words seems unending. If Christ wins this battle against our self-life, He becomes the center of our personalities, and we become Christ-centered. The happy consequence of a Christ-centered life is the manifestation of the fruit of the Spirit.

The nature of fruitfulness

The principle of fruit bearing is a "life principle." Life develops from a life source; it cannot be manufactured. Fruit is not made; it grows as the requirements of the life principle are met. In contrast, the works of the flesh as described in the Scriptures are a negative result of human effort without the Holy Spirit. Samuel Chadwick, referring to Galatians 5:19–21, observed:

> The most striking feature of this contrast is its emphatic change from works to fruit. Work belongs to the workshop; fruit belongs to the garden. One comes from the ingenuity of the factory; the other is the silent growth of an abounding life. The factory operates with dead stuff; the garden cultivates a living force to their appointed end. Works are always in the realm of dead things. Every building is built out of dead material. A tree must die before it can be used by the builder. There is no life

in stones and brick and steel joints and iron girders. They are all dead and in the process of disintegration. No earthly material lasts. Man's best works fail and fade and crumble and pass away. Fruit does not come of man's labor. It requires his diligence, but it is neither his invention nor his product. He does not make the flowers. No skill of his brings the golden harvest of the fields or the lush fruit of the trees. When man has done all he can do, then God begins and life proceeds. Fruit is God's work. The phrase "fruit of the Spirit" assigns the graces of the Christian character to their proper source. They are not of man's producing.[2]

The Scriptures clearly teach the life-principle involved in bearing fruit. The flesh can produce nothing but evil works, while the Holy Spirit produces Christ-life fruit. The former requires self-effort and results in death; the latter requires obedience to the Holy Spirit and produces life and peace.

The source of fruitfulness

How does the Holy Spirit work in our lives to produce the fruit of a Christ-life character? The psalmist described the "blessed man" as a tree planted by the river of water that yields its fruit in its season (Ps. 1:3). He declares of this fruitful life that "his delight is in the law of the LORD, and in His law he meditates day and night" (v. 2, NAS). The place that we give the Word of God in our lives will determine our degree of fruitfulness.

Meditation. David doesn't say that this blessed man simply reads the Word. He *meditates* on it as well. We find the admonition to stop and meditate given throughout the Book of Psalms. The word *selah* found in many of the psalms means to meditate, to stop and think about what has been said. A word picture of *selah* is the cow chewing her cud after eating to assimilate all she has swallowed. As we read and meditate on the Scriptures, the Holy Spirit can convince us of sin that needs to be purged and can direct us to God's standard of holiness and righteousness for our lives. Apart from applying the Word of God, there can be no lasting spiritual growth and no fruit-bearing in our lives.

Spiritual disciplines. We have discussed the abiding principle that Jesus taught the disciples as a prerequisite for bearing fruit (John 15). Truly abiding in the vine will result in an intimate relationship with Christ, allowing nothing to separate us from Him. We need to give ourselves to disciplines in our lives that will help cultivate this abiding relationship. These disciplines include not only giving ourselves to searching the Word of God, but also *hearing* the Word that is lifed by anointed preaching, as well as spending much time in *prayer* and *worship* in the Spirit. These help us feed our inner man on His life and help grace us in our relationship with Him. *Fellowship* with other believers is also an important spiritual discipline because it allows us to commune with Christ and to participate in His life indirectly, through each other. Jesus was emphatic that we can only bear spiritual fruit if we abide in Him. The life of Christ, as the life-giving sap in the vine, is essential to spiritual growth and fruit bearing.

Obedience. The secret to abiding in Christ is to (a) *believe* in our spirits; (b) *obey* in our souls; and (c) *yield* our flesh to the power of the Holy Spirit. This abiding obedience involves every aspect of our person. *Obedience* is a word we sometimes don't like to hear. It seems almost an obsolete word in Christendom. We hear much about faith but so little about obedience. But Jesus said, "If you keep My commandments, you will abide in My love" (John 15:10, NAS). Obedience brings maturity and develops the fruit of the Spirit in our lives. We cannot display the fruit of the Spirit when sin or neglect has interrupted our fellowship with Christ.

I knew a woman who was a faithful reader of the Word, and her life evidenced it by the fruit she was bearing. But for some reason she neglected her study of the Word for three or four days, and she began to be irritable and impatient. Her little four-year-old daughter observed her mother's reactions for a day, and then said to her, "Mother, why don't you get into the Word?" That four-year-old child understood Jesus's command better than most of us. As we learn to abide in the true vine, His life flows into us, producing the fruit of the Spirit to the Father's glory and to the blessing of others.

Some things about our relationship with Christ we may not fully understand. Suppose we were to ask a branch on a grapevine, "How do you grow luscious fruit?" If the branch could talk, it probably would say, "I don't know. I don't grow any of it; I just bear it. If you cut me away from this vine, I will just wither away and become useless." Just as without the vine the branch can produce nothing, so it is in our Christian lives. If we strain to work to produce the fruit of the Spirit ourselves, we will find ourselves fruitless and frustrated.

But if we abide in Christ, maintaining a close, obedient, dependent relationship with Him, God the Holy Spirit can work in us, creating and producing the fruit of the Spirit. The manifestation of that fruit in our lives, as we have seen, is the life of the Lord Jesus in His godly character of holiness. This doesn't mean that we instantly become mature, bearing all the fruit of the Spirit fully and immediately. Even after fruit appears on the tree, it takes time—time during which the elements of wind and rain and even storms bring the fruit to maturity. This desired maturity is impossible without our continually abiding in the vine.

We should understand also that receiving the baptism of the Holy Spirit does not automatically result in the fruit of the Spirit being formed in our lives. One who has yielded his life more fully to the Holy Spirit in receiving the baptism of the Holy Spirit will obviously have the divine enabling to develop *more* fruit, *much* fruit, and fruit that *remains*. However, every believer who has accepted Christ as Savior has the Holy Spirit abiding in him. As he continues to abide in Christ, he will experience the fruit of the Spirit in his life.

Because fruit bearing is a direct result of abiding in Christ, there are deeply spiritual and fruitful Christians who have never had evidence of having received the Pentecostal experience of Holy Spirit baptism. On the other hand it is sadly true that there are Spirit-baptized Christians who have not developed the fruit of the Spirit to any degree in their lives through consciously abiding in Christ. Both cases prove the reality that fruitfulness is not a result of receiving the baptism of the Holy Spirit, but is a result of abiding in Christ. It remains, then, that the key to the quantity and quality of fruitfulness in our lives is abiding in Christ, the Vine, in obedience to His commands.

The apostle Paul addressed the Galatians and the Corinthians concerning these issues, for many of them had received the baptism of the Holy Spirit but were still void of Christ's love. Some of these early Christians placed their priorities on the gifts of the Spirit operating through them. I have known some Pentecostal Christians who suppose that the baptism in the Holy Spirit as a single experience is the crowning attainment of the Christian life. That is not true. The real crowning attainment for any Christian is to live a Spirit-filled and Spirit-led life daily, abounding in the fruit of the Spirit.

If the Holy Spirit who abides in us is hindered, grieved, and quenched while we sow to the flesh instead of yielding to the Spirit, we can expect to live a fruitless life. It is an immutable divine law that whatever we sow, we will also reap (Gal. 6:7).

We cannot overestimate the importance of abiding in the vine. Jesus taught His disciples the consequences for living otherwise: "Every branch in Me that bears no fruit, He takes away" (John 15:2). What does He do with it? "If anyone does not abide in Me, he is thrown away as a branch, and dries up; and they gather them, and cast them into the fire and they are burned" (v. 6, NAS). It is not the vine that is rejected, but the fruitless branch. If the branches are removed and cast into the fire, it is because they bear no fruit.

This judgment applies to born-again Christians, not mere professing believers. The expression "every branch in Me" clearly shows that some who are taken away for failing to produce fruit had once been true branches in the vine. Even though they were branches, having received life from the vine, they did not continue to abide in the vine and failed to produce fruit. It is my earnest conviction that what God requires He provides, and I believe what He provides He requires. As applied here, that means that God provides the life, the sap, and the elements necessary to the branch, and therefore He has a right to expect fruitfulness of the believer.

Pruning process

If one does not abide in Christ, he cannot bear fruit and, according to Jesus's teaching, will be cast away. If a branch does bear fruit, the requirement made of the fruitful branch is that it endure purging. Listen to Jesus's words: "And every branch that bears fruit, He prunes, that it may bear more fruit"

(John 15:2). This suggests the process of pruning or cutting away some areas in our lives that were once fruitful.

The primary purpose of pruning a vine is to remove the wood that produced fruit last season to force the vine to grow new wood that will produce fruit. God does not perpetuate the old; He prunes to force new growth. If we have experienced some pruning in our lives, it is not because God is mad at us, or that there is necessarily sin in our lives. It is that the Father is pleased we are bearing fruit, and He knows that to increase the quality and quantity of that fruit, we need to be pruned. Pruning to the Christian is never pleasant; it suggests chastening. Sometimes the enemy whispers his suggestions to us that it is punishment. However, there is a vast difference between correction or chastening, and punishment. The former belongs to the family of God and works redemption in us; the latter belongs to Satan and his angels.

The Scriptures teach that although "no discipline seems to be joyful at the time, but grievous. Yet afterward it yields the peaceful fruit of righteousness..." (Heb. 12:11). God's goal in our lives is to produce fruit. He knows that at times the pruning knife is necessary to cut away the excess of "flesh" and strengthen the root so more fruit can be produced. Leaves and foliage can be very beautiful. In the spring season I can look out in the yard, and the trees are verdant, luscious, and lively. However, there is no fruit yet. Sometimes when the Master comes, He doesn't even find fruit when it is past the time that fruit should have been produced. So He must cut away the leaves of self-indulgence from our lives so we can bear His fruit.

Jesus continued, "My Father is glorified by this, that you bear much fruit..." (John 15:8). Lest we should tend to draw back from this painful pruning process, He admonishes us to remember that our Father is the Husbandman (John 15:1). He is the one who holds the knife, not man. We can safely trust ourselves to His loving care. If we had to submit to someone who didn't understand the vine, didn't know how to prune it, and caused it to bleed and die, we might have a reason to be uneasy. However, our heavenly Father is the Master Husbandman, and He holds the pruning instrument in His hand. We may ask what He uses for a knife. It is His Word, which is "sharper than any two-edged sword, piercing even to the division of soul and spirit…and able to judge the thoughts and intents of the heart" (Heb. 4:12).

It is comforting in our seasons of pruning to remember how close the Father must be as He does His meticulous purging work. He will never ask other people to use the pruning shears on His vines. Sometimes I feel that some ministers try to prune the branches in their churches; but that is not God's way. Ministers are to water and care for the branches. The pruning is not left to man; it is God's work. So every branch that abides in Christ and is an integral part of the vine must never be severed from that vine. If it is, it will die. We must never allow anything to come between our source of life and ourselves.

There is no better way for our lives to be pruned than through studying the Word and applying it to our hearts, walking in obedience, and yielding to what the Holy Spirit reveals to us. In that way pruning becomes a natural result of abiding in the vine as we described earlier. When Jesus spoke of pruning, He said, "You are already clean because of the word which I have spoken to you" (John 15:3, NAS). The Greek root word used here for clean can be translated *pruned*. One version translates this verse, "Now, you have already been pruned by my words" (John 15:3, PHILLIPS). If we abide in His

Word, the Holy Spirit can correct us and tell us where we have fallen short and gone astray.

The Holy Spirit doesn't discourage us or condemn us; He convicts us. That means He uses the Word to point out our problem with a desire to correct it. He always has the solution. If abiding is the primary condition God sets before us to bear the fruit of the Spirit, then why do we seek to be fruitful in other ways? Why is it that the simplicity of God's way is always the way that seems so difficult for the flesh? It is, according to the Scriptures, because our spirits and our flesh are at war. Our flesh opposes the desire of the Holy Spirit to make us holy because it does not want to die. If there is sin in our lives, if there is a lack of discipline, or a broken relationship with our Lord or others, in order to abide in Christ we need to confess our sin or shortcoming and forgive others. In whatever way the works of flesh are controlling us, causing us to live in unrighteousness, we need to bring it to Christ in confession and repentance as the Holy Spirit convicts us. He will forgive us, purge us, and enable us to live the Christ-life, bearing the fruit of His character by the "lifing" of the Holy Spirit.

As we cultivate a fruitful relationship in Christ by spending time reading and meditating on God's Word and in prayer, the Holy Spirit continually reveals truth to us. Then as we walk in obedience to that truth instead of obeying our fleshly desires, the Holy Spirit transforms us, and we begin to bring forth His fruit by the power of the Spirit. Every believer must have an unbroken relationship with Christ sustained by obedience. In unwavering faith in what Christ has done, we must acknowledge Him as the Vine and His Father as the Husbandman, the divine Pruner.

Our obedience will cause us also to be continually rejoicing in our Lord as we realize that we are redeemed and justified and are children of God. We are heirs of God, and He has preordained, foreordained, and predestined that we bear fruit. This conscious fellowship with our Lord will cause us to be fruit-bearing trees. There ought to be an ever-increasing diligence to yield to the Holy Spirit, to obey His commands, and to walk in His will so we may be fruitful. That is why Paul taught that we must live in the Spirit, be led by the Spirit, and walk in the Spirit (Gal. 5).

THE GIFTS AND FRUIT CONTRASTED

We hear much about the gifts of the Spirit these days. Many people are enamored with the supernatural power that can flow through a Spirit-filled believer. For that reason it is important to remember that spiritual gifts are only supernatural capabilities given by the Holy Spirit, while the fruit of the Spirit is godly character. The gifts of the Spirit equip one with abilities for service in the kingdom of God; the fruit of the Spirit reveals who one is in the kingdom of God. It may be possible for us to function in the gifts of the Spirit even when we are not abiding in Christ as we should.

The Scriptures teach that fruit-bearing, rather than functioning in the gifts of the Spirit, is an indication of maturity and spirituality. Although there is a tendency among us to look with awe on someone who has many gifts of the Spirit, Paul clearly teaches that the gifts are not an indication of the depth of one's spiritual life. He wrote to the Corinthians whom, he said, "are not lacking in any gift" (1 Cor. 1:7), and corrected them for being carnal, unspiritual people. The gifts are given instantaneously because of our yielding in obedience to the Holy Spirit. Fruit is not produced instantaneously; it is the result of our abiding in Christ and develops gradually. In fruit-bearing, developing traits of godly character requires *time*, *testings*, and *trials*.

In the Old Testament supernatural gifts did not suggest spirituality either. King Saul was noted for his possession of the gift of prophecy. The people asked the question, "Is Saul also among the prophets?" (1 Sam. 10:11). They had heard him prophesy with other prophets. Later during his reign as king he dishonored the Lord, disobeyed His Word, and God no longer heard his prayers. The Spirit of the Lord even departed from him. It is obvious from this example and others that the development of godly character, not the operation of spiritual gifts, is the real indication of relationship with God.

Another way we might consider the difference between the fruit of the Spirit and the gifts of the Spirit is that gifts are plural, but fruit is not. As we have seen, there are varieties of spiritual gifts given by the Spirit for the edifying of the church. All my Christian life I have heard people use the plural form of the word *fruit*, referring to the "nine fruits" of the Spirit. However, Paul used a singular verb, *is*, to describe the fruit of the Spirit. For example, *love* is the single channel through which the fruit of the Spirit flows. Paul then describes the other eight characteristics or facets of divine love, the fruit of the Spirit, as evidenced in the Christian's life by the power of the Holy Spirit. Paul taught that "the love of God is shed abroad in our hearts by the Holy Spirit..." (Rom. 5:5). So the fruit of love works in our lives and manifests its beauty in eight different ways. D. L. Moody described the fruit of the Spirit this way:

> Joy is love exulting; peace is love reposing; longsuffering
> is love untiring; gentleness is love enduring; goodness is

love in action; faith is love on the battlefield; meekness
is love under discipline; temperance is love in training.[3]

We know that we are continually being filled with the
Holy Spirit if we are manifesting the love of God in its many
facets in our lives.

The apostle Paul teaches clearly that the gifts of the Spirit,
administered without love, profit nothing to the one administering them. Amazingly he went as far as to say that those
who function in spiritual gifts are nothing without love. He
begins the "love chapter" by declaring, "If I speak with the
tongues of men and of angels, and have not love, I have become
as sounding brass or a clanging cymbal" (1 Cor. 13:1). He continued to list the spiritual gifts we hold in awe and declared
that if he had them all but did not have love, he was nothing.
Although Paul was not inferring that the gifts were useless
when administered through a loveless channel, he did say, "it
profits me nothing" (v. 3). The one administering the gifts
without love is the loser, not the church.

Unfortunately many Christians today, in their pursuit of
charisma, anointing, power, and the gifts of the Spirit, have
forsaken the building of character in their lives. Because of a
lack of character in Christians' lives, there has been a dimin-
ishing of power in the body of Christ. Why? The love of God
is the channel through which His power flows. Ministered in
love through a fruitful, spiritual life, the gifts of the Spirit are
of great usefulness and great power in building the kingdom of
our Lord. We must conclude that the Holy Spirit is as much
interested in character as He is in power.

What would happen if a pastor gave an altar call and asked
all who wanted holiness and the character of God to come forward and stand on the left side of the altar? If he then asked all

who wanted the gifts of power of the Holy Spirit to come forward and stand on the right side, I believe the larger portion of his church would be on the right side. Those desiring power would be the majority, with maybe a handful seeking character. People want power. There is something in every one of us that wants to be in control. But every Spirit-baptized servant of the Lord needs to realize the importance of godly character, especially as it relates to the gifts of the Spirit. It is most important that the life of our Lord Jesus is recognized in us as the vine that produces fruit in our lives.

THE FRUITS AND GIFTS COMPARED

Having contrasted the spiritual gifts and fruit, let's not fail to realize, however, the vital relationship they share in common. It is not by chance nor a departure from true canonicity for the Holy Spirit to place the "love chapter" (1 Cor. 13) between the chapters dealing with the proper use of the gifts of the Spirit (1 Cor. 12; 14). My dear friend Dr. Judson Cornwall keenly observed that even though the contrasts between the gifts of the Spirit and the fruit of the Spirit are great, there are at least two comparisons. First, both flow from the Holy Spirit into and through the lives of persons in whom the Spirit dwells. There is a common divine Source, even though there is an uncommon result. A second similarity is that both the gifts of the Spirit and the fruit of the Spirit are listed for us in the Bible in groups of three. In our study of the nine gifts of the Spirit listed in 1 Corinthians 12, we saw three gifts that supernaturally enable us to know, three that supernaturally enable us to do, and three that supernaturally enable us to speak. We have noted that the fruit of the Spirit, in essence, is love. However, the aspects of love, relating to their effect on our relationships, logically divide into three clusters as well. The first cluster—love, joy, peace—ripens toward God. The second cluster ripens toward others—long-suffering, gentleness, goodness. The third cluster, those aspects of love that grow in the shade of the vine, ripen toward ourselves—meekness, faithfulness, temperance. As the fruit of love develops in these three dimensions in our lives, we will bear the character of Christ.

As we begin to study the fruit of love with its eight characteristic facets, we might consider whether our priority has been to have the gifts of the Spirit or to develop godly character. If we recognize a lack in our lives of the love of God, though we are functioning in the gifts of the Spirit, we need to acknowledge that lack. As we learn to abide in Christ, we will become effective in building the kingdom of God. Then we will avoid the terrible prospect of becoming a clanging cymbal, or worse, a branch that must be taken away and burned. Should we not desire to dwell continually in the love of God where we are not only safe from our enemies, but fruitful as well?

Chapter 7

The Fruit of the Spirit

Part II:
Divine Love, Joy, Peace,
Long-Suffering, and Gentleness

. . . .

Remain in Me, as I also remain in you. As the branch
cannot bear fruit by itself, unless it remains in the
vine, neither can you, unless you remain in Me.

—JOHN 15:4

. . . .

LOVE

But the fruit of the Spirit is love…

—GALATIANS 5:22

*L*OVE MUST HAVE preeminence in the virtues of
the Christian life because God is love. John wrote,
"Beloved, let us love one another, for love is of God, and
everyone who loves is born of God and knows God" (1 John
4:7). Throughout his epistle John emphasizes that love is the
evidence of true relationship with God. Jesus taught His disciples: "By this all men will know that you are My disciples,

if you have love for one another" (John 13:35). If the disciples thought it difficult to love one another, they must have cringed at the other command Jesus gave concerning love. He said, "Love your enemies, bless those who curse you, do good to those who hate you, and pray for those who spitefully use you and persecute you" (Matt. 5:44).

This command to love our enemies is impossible for the natural man to fulfill. This fruit cannot be produced by human effort; it is the result of the love of God Himself being shed abroad in our hearts. The love that the Holy Spirit produces is much more than ordinary human affection. It is God's very character—who He is. It is that love flowing through our spirits into our souls, and made manifest through our human flesh, that the Holy Spirit produces. It is only the love of God that will enable us to love our enemies.

Among all the words in the Bible, this simple word *love* stands alone as the supreme description of the very essence of the Christian life. Love binds all other virtues of the fruit of the Spirit together. It is the common denominator of Christian character. One cannot love completely and fail to cultivate the other virtues. To be filled with the Holy Spirit and display the fruit of the Spirit in our lives is to be filled with love. One might ask, "Why is love of supreme importance?" Many reasons could be given. Let's examine some of them.

THE SIGNIFICANCE OF LOVE

God is love.

First, the Scriptures teach that love is not just one of God's attributes, but the very essence of His being. We must remember that God is love, He doesn't have love. There is a real difference between what one has and who one is. All true love finds its origin in God and flows forth from Him. God intended that love, the essence of who He is, would be the essence of His creation as well. All redemption is designed to restore this reality of God's intention for a loving creation.

Motive for creation

Second, love is so important because it was the motive for all creation. This God of love needed someone to respond to His love. Because of that need God created mankind as an object of His love, to share His life, His wisdom, His holiness, His character, His eternal riches, and ultimately His glory. Even before the foundation of the world, God in His omniscience knew that man would fail. So God made a provision for the devil's interruption that tried to destroy His plan to have a human family He could love. God demonstrated His love to us in that He provided the remedy for that interruption even before He made man. The Scriptures teach that Jesus was "the Lamb who was slain from the foundation of the world" (Rev. 13:8).[1] After God made man, man's choice to disobey God resulted in a broken relationship with God. Yet God's love continued to reach out to him, so that "while we were yet sinners, Christ died for us" (Rom. 5:8). What incredible love! God's love for us is unconditional and undeserved. He loves us in spite of ourselves.

Fulfilling of the Law

Third, love is of supreme importance because it is the greatest commandment that fulfills all the Law of God. When the scribe asked Jesus which of the commandments was the greatest, He replied:

"You shall love the Lord your God with all your heart, and with all your soul, and with all your mind." This is the first and great commandment. And the second is like it: "You shall love your neighbor as yourself." On these two commandments hang all the Law and the Prophets.

—MATTHEW 22:37–40

You remember that the Law was written on two tablets of stone. The first four commandments are regarding our love for God and God only, and the last six deal with our relationship to man, loving our neighbor. Therefore, Paul declared that "love is the fulfilling of the law" (Rom. 13:10, KJV).

Our sure sign of discipleship

Fourth, Jesus gave His disciples a new commandment to love one another. He declared, "By this all men will know that you are My disciples, if you have love for one another" (John 13:35). Our doctrine should be sound, and our faith should be strong. Still, those are not signs of our testimony to the world that we are disciples of Christ. According to the Scriptures, only God's *agape* love manifested in our lives is the sure sign that we are His disciples. For that reason love must be foundational in our lives, motivating everything we do. Paul admonished believers to follow the way of love (1 Cor. 14:1), and to do everything with love (1 Cor. 16:14).

The principle of love

If I speak with the tongues of men and of angels, and have not love, I have become as sounding brass or a clanging cymbal. If I have the gift of prophecy, and understand all mysteries and all knowledge, and if I have all faith, so that I could remove mountains, and

have not love, I am nothing. If I give all my goods to feed
the poor, and if I give my body to be burned, and have
not love, it profits me nothing.

—1 CORINTHIANS 13:1–3

Since love is of supreme importance in our spiritual lives,
we need to understand the principle of love as it is outlined in
the Scriptures. The love Paul describes is selfless rather than
selfish; it is a supernatural love operating through us, not the
love of our self-efforts or natural affections. The Charismatic
movement emphasized (a) tongues; (b) the gifts of the Spirit;
(c) faith to move mountains; and (d) giving. In the "love chapter"
Paul mentions all four of these areas of emphasis, contrasting
them with the need for love. What is the Holy Spirit saying
here? He is saying that even in the Charismatic movement, if
we have all these supernatural endowments and do not have
love, they are of no value to us.

The Bible teaches that our goal must be to put love first.
The apostle John writes more about this: "And we have come to
know and to believe the love that God has for us. God is love.
Whoever lives in love lives in God, and God in him" (1 John
4:16). We would do well to meditate on that powerful statement, "Whoever lives in love lives in God, and God in him."
Where do true anointing, power, and faith come from? Don't
they come from dwelling in God? And dwelling in God means
dwelling in love. Are we as Spirit-filled Christians aiming
simply for gifts, power, anointing, and faith—or the love that
produces these things? God will show up wherever love shows
up. A person who dwells in love brings the presence of God to
every life situation.

We have established that the fruit of the Spirit is the love
of God developed in the believer. Now we are ready to study

the other aspects or facets of this supernatural fruit that are descriptive of it. As we gain understanding of the characteristics of each virtue, we will be able to recognize them practically and make them operative in our life circumstances. The Scriptures offer us simple guidelines to show us how to allow each of these virtues to be manifested in our lives. As we yield to the Holy Spirit, He will cultivate His fruit in us and allow us to experience the love of God as He intended.

Joy

> I say these things in the world, that they may have My joy fulfilled in themselves.
> —John 17:13

The joy that comes from the Holy Spirit as He produces the character of our Lord in us can range in emotional response from a sense of well-being, tranquility, or quietness, to an exuberant gladness. That gladness can be expressed in singing, clapping, dancing, and even loud victory cheers. Whatever our response, we must remember that only the Holy Spirit can produce true joy in our lives. It will never be manufactured by our efforts.

I remember when I first came into the Spirit-filled walk, I would hear the church sing a lively chorus called, "The Joy of the Lord Is My Strength." One verse declared, "If you want joy you must clap for it, dance for it, shout for it." As we went through all those motions, I finally realized we were trying to work up joy by our own efforts: clapping, dancing, and shouting. Somehow we got the idea that if we did these things, we would have joy from God and then we would have strength.

I didn't understand then that God Himself is true joy. True joy is part of the character of Christ. So since joy is part of God's nature and part of Christ's life, we become heirs to this joy as we allow His nature to be developed in us. "For the kingdom of God does not mean eating and drinking, but righteousness and peace and joy in the Holy Spirit" (Rom. 14:17). True joy, then, is love's response to God's mercies, His blessings, and His benefits.

The joy of the Christian is not dependent on circumstances. It is not our environment, the people around us, or the events we are going through that determine our joy or lack of it. This divine joy lives in trust even in the most trying circumstances. Human happiness looks at things on the earth and is affected by its conditions—what is going on around it. But divine joy, as part of the fruit of love, looks heavenward. It is unaffected by people, events, or surrounding conditions because heaven's benefits are unchanging.

The genuine Christian will express the emotion of joy. David declared, "In Your presence is fullness of joy" (Ps. 16:11). Those who would suppress all expression of emotion in worship, condemning enthusiasm and rejoicing as emotionalism, do not rightly interpret the Word of God. Emotionalism, which is to be avoided, is the seeking of emotion as an end: emotion for emotion's sake. We carefully differentiate between emotional extravagance and the true operation of the Holy Spirit in our emotions. In keeping with the teaching of the Scriptures, we exercise self-control over our feelings so as not to grasp selfishly for attention in our emotional experiences.

On the other hand, we believe in singing joyfully, praying earnestly, preaching zealously, testifying forcefully, and giving cheerfully. Not one sentence of condemnation for enthusiasm and rejoicing can be found in God's Word. The Scriptures are full of commands to rejoice, to shout, to dance, and to sing unto God. Paul uses the words *joy* and *rejoice* seventeen times in his short epistle to the Philippians. Emotionless worship is cold worship. Joy is an expression of godly emotion in the inner being that is inwardly moved by love for God. The joy of the Lord is our strength, and as the Spirit of the Lord fills a person, joy will be manifest in his or her life.

Years ago we buried the last member of my immediate family, my only brother. His death left me without family: mother, daddy, grandfather, grandmother, aunt, uncle, or brother. When it dawned on me that I didn't have a birthplace or family to go back to, an emptiness and loneliness settled in my spirit that pierced me deeply. Just as I was experiencing that deep pain, I heard a song inside my spirit. A line from an old hymn that declared the Comforter had come was running through my mind. I looked up at my husband and said, "Honey, the Comforter I preach about is now comforting me." In the midst of my pain, despite my loss, I could still experience the comfort and joy of the presence of the Lord. You might ask, "Did you feel like singing and dancing?" No. I was grieving. But I realized that nothing in this world could steal what I had inside: the comforting presence of God that is so eternal. Even though I was walking through the valley, my God was with me, and in that fact I could rejoice. I didn't have to go through the seven steps some prescribe for resolving grief because the joy of His presence brought infinite peace.

It is true that life is sometimes painful and that we do not always have answers for the difficulties we encounter. In those times I have discovered that true joy doesn't depend on our outward circumstances, but on our inward responses to God and to those circumstances. When we learn to see our lives from God's perspective, we can draw on the strength that comes from His joy.

Joy in heaven

Jesus said, "Likewise, I tell you, there will be more joy in heaven over one sinner who repents than over ninety-nine righteous men who need no repentance" (Luke 15:7). Melody Green, a saintly woman and dear friend, made this observation concerning Jesus's statement: "Think of it! The joyful angelic outburst must be like celestial fireworks when people on earth become reconciled to God. All heaven has a display of heavenly fireworks because of the joy of the Lord they experience when a son has come home!"[2]

The Old Testament prophet declared, "The LORD your God is in your midst, a Mighty One, who will save. He will rejoice over you with gladness, He will renew you with His love, He will rejoice over you with singing" (Zeph. 3:17). The Hebrew word for *rejoice* literally means "to spin around exultantly." So God rejoices over His people with dancing, with singing, and with shouts of joy. The Lord on His heavenly throne is not blind or unfeeling toward the suffering, injustice, and sin on the earth. Yet overriding joy grips Him when one soul is delivered from the chains of sin and the grip of death.

On the Day of Pentecost in Peter's first sermon he quoted David, saying, "Thou hast made known to me the ways of life; Thou shalt make me full of joy with thy countenance" (Acts 2:28, KJV). Just to see the countenance of the Lord fills us with joy. Joy was a characteristic of the disciples who were full of the Holy Spirit, even as they faced persecution (Acts 13:50–52). I have seen that when believers today are baptized in the Holy Spirit, they too experience a baptism of the joy of the Lord. I believe this great release of joy is a result of the dynamic overflowing of the Spirit of God when He takes up full residence within us, establishing His purposes in our lives. What a wonder it is that God has made a way for us to become like

Him! Surely this should be our highest priority in life, to allow the love of God to dwell in us so we become joyful ambassadors of His kingdom of love here on earth.

PEACE

> But now in Christ Jesus you who were formerly far away
> have been brought near by the blood of Christ.
> —EPHESIANS 2:13–14

I had a beautiful experience that defined peace for me. I was taking a group of young people through Natural Bridge, Virginia, sometimes listed as one of the Seven Wonders of the World. We were touring deep underground in the Endless Caverns. As we walked through those deep caves, we came to a ridge that was like a mountain underneath the ground. From that ridge we looked down into a deep ravine through which flowed the clearest stream of water I had ever seen. It looked as though it might be several feet deep, and it was running its own course—so tranquil, so undisturbed, so unaware of being walked over by the tourists above it.

As I stood there, the Holy Spirit whispered to my spirit and said, "This is peace like a river—the peace of God that passes understanding." I realized when I saw that natural example of peacefulness that there could be a river of peace inside me coming from the life of the Lord Jesus, a river that is fuller and deeper and in much greater harmony with God than anything this world could offer. No wonder the apostle Paul used the Greek word *symphoneos*, from which we derive our word *symphony*, to describe this peace that brings us into perfect harmony with God, without any discord.

Peace can be defined as a soul-harmony that comes from the Christ-rule living within us. This divine peace is an experience that is much deeper and more constant than happiness. This beautiful facet of love is an inner characteristic that manifests itself in peaceableness with God, with others, and with ourselves. It signifies freedom from an agitated, contentious, or quarrelsome spirit. Love seeks to live peaceably with all men. The Spirit-filled believer may enjoy this peace that is described in the Scriptures.

Four aspects of peace

The Word of God teaches four different aspects of divine peace that we may experience in our relationship with our Lord. First, we can have peace with God (Rom. 5:1). This peace means the war is over in our spirits. We are not warring anymore with our conscience or with God. We have declared our armistice and have been reconciled to God through repenting of our sins and accepting the sacrifice of Jesus's blood to cover them. This born-again experience results in peace with God.

Second, there is peace *from* God. When Jesus was preparing His disciples for His death, He said, "Peace I leave with you. My peace I give to you. Not as the world gives do I give to you. Let not your heart be troubled, neither let it be afraid" (John 14:27). This aspect of peace focuses on the gift of God. Paul called peace a gift of God when he declared, "He is our peace" (Eph. 2:14). Jesus is the Prince of Peace. Therefore, if He is living in us, producing His life through us by the power of the Holy Spirit, then it is His peace that sustains us and keeps us from inward turmoil. We experience a divine peace that is not a result of any human effort.

Third, the Scriptures describe the peace *of* God. Paul told the Philippians, "And the peace of God, which surpasses all understanding, will protect your hearts and minds through Christ Jesus" (Phil. 4:7). In his salutation to the Thessalonians he prayed, "Now may the Lord of peace Himself give you peace always in every way" (2 Thess. 3:16). This is a description essential to God's divine love: "peace always." He desires that we enjoy that peaceful state as we experience His love. The dynamic power of this peace is expressed in the phrase "peace that surpasses all understanding." No matter what kind of vexing situation or painful circumstance we have to face, we can go through it in the power of the Holy Spirit in the peace of God that is not dependent on our natural ability to cope.

Fourth, the prophet Isaiah referred to perfect peace *in* Him. He wrote, "You will keep him in perfect peace, whose mind is stayed on You, because he trusts in You" (Isa. 26:3). This aspect of peace describes that abiding relationship that comes as our minds are "stayed" on God. The Hebrew word for *stayed* carries the connotation of "nailing down securely." As our minds are nailed down on Christ, because of our trust in Him, He will keep us in perfect peace. That peace that is a fruit of divine love is real and genuine. The common greeting among the Jewish people was "Shalom," or "Peace." We will be at home in peace. May He who comes to look for fruit on our branches find peace growing profusely in the garden of our lives.

LONG-SUFFERING

But the fruit of the Spirit is…longsuffering…
—GALATIANS 5:22, KJV

…giving all diligence, add to your faith virtue; and to virtue knowledge; and to knowledge temperance; and to temperance patience; and to patience godliness; and to godliness brotherly kindness; and to brotherly kindness charity.
—2 PETER 1:5–7, KJV

Although long-suffering, otherwise translated as patience, is a lost virtue among many Christians today, it is essential to the Christian walk. We have established the fact that the fruit of the Spirit is Christlike character, not the fruit of our own efforts. It is so with patience also; this godly aspect of character will be a "natural" result of a life that is controlled supernaturally by the Spirit of Christ.

Still, we must remember that the development of godly fruit is neither automatic nor instantaneous. Christlike character doesn't develop without diligence on the believer's part to yield continually to the Holy Spirit in each situation he confronts in life. The Greek word Peter used for patience can also be translated *perseverance*. This desirable fruit will only be brought forth by much prayer, study of God's Word, and perseverance in life's difficulties. Patience is the ability to endure graciously a less-than-desired state for an extended time.

James understood this when he wrote, "As an example, brethren, of suffering and patience, take the prophets who spoke in the name of the Lord. We count those blessed who endured" (James 5:10–11, NAS). James informs us that we develop patience through a process of endurance and determined struggle. Paul declared, "For I have learned in whatever state I am to be content" (Phil. 4:11). He learned contentment in life's less-than-desirable situations. In that statement he confirms that contentment is a learned virtue that must be developed.

Paul also prayed for the Colossians that they would be "strengthened with all power, according to His glorious might, for the attaining of all steadfastness and patience; joyously giving thanks to the Father" (Col. 1:11–12, NAS). Because patience is not an option for the Spirit-filled Christian, but a necessary virtue, we must cultivate it through prayer and surrender to the working of God's power within us.

The Scriptures give several reasons for the need to develop patience in our lives. For example, Paul told Timothy that patience should characterize the way we share the gospel. He wrote, "Preach the word; be ready in season and out of season; reprove, rebuke, exhort, with great patience and instruction" (2 Tim. 4:2, NAS). Second, patience is a key to receiving God's promises. The Scriptures teach, "So that you may not be lazy, but imitators of those who through faith and patience inherit the promises" (Heb. 6:12). Perhaps one of the greatest reasons we need to have patience is that through testings that produce patience, Christian character is perfected. James declared, "But let patience perfect its work, that you may be perfect and complete, lacking nothing" (James 1:4). He also taught us that patience is the pathway to blessing: "We count those blessed who endured" (James 5:11, NAS).

Waiting patiently

A most difficult aspect of patience involves waiting. Waiting is something very few of us want to do, like to do, or can do. Most people consider waiting to be a negative experience. Yet true success is usually determined by how a person uses such waiting periods. What we may think is a time of adversity and "standstill" could be God's time element of preparation in our lives for a task for which we are not yet ready. The manifestation of patience, such as the manifestation of other traits of godly character, may be seen in a single act, but the development of each is the result of many testings and trials. The character we develop as we respond properly in our trials may well be the preventative of failure in the future. Jesus declared, "In your patience possess ye your souls" (Luke 21:19, KJV).

A distressed king by the name of Jehoram once asked the prophet Elisha, "Why should I wait for the LORD any longer?" (2 Kings 6:33, NAS). Many who are sick, economically deprived, tempted, abused, stressed, or otherwise unhappy, are asking the same question today: "How long, O Lord, how long? Why should I wait for the Lord to deliver me?" Elisha encouraged King Jehoram and charged the people to trust God and wait for their supernatural deliverance. That very night God drove the enemies away and gave His people all the food and treasure they needed from the enemy's camp. Even when the situation looks hopeless, patience does not surrender to despair. We need to persevere and be patient as we wait for the Lord, knowing that our deliverance will surely come. Though patience may be a lost virtue for many, it is part of the character of the fruit of the Spirit that should be predominant in our Christian lives.

GENTLENESS

> But the wisdom that is from above is first pure, then peaceable, gentle, open to reason, full of mercy and good fruits, without partiality, and without hypocrisy.
>
> —JAMES 3:17

Even though the Scriptures use the word *gentleness* in other places, the only time this Greek word is found in the New Testament is when Paul describes the fruit of the Spirit (Gal. 5:22–23). It is the word we use for kindness and frequently depicts God's dealings with His people. Gentleness, or kindness, is Christ's tangible expression of His love in our lives. Jesus said of Himself, "I am gentle and humble in heart" (Matt. 11:29, NAS). Gentleness beautifully characterizes the love of our Savior for rebellious sinners.

Few words are so easily defined as *kindness*. For most people, this aspect of the fruit of the Spirit can be defined with words such as *caring, mercy, compassion,* and *concern,* along with other words that express warmth of feeling toward another person. Only the meanest of "schoolyard bullies" would not aspire to possess and exhibit these qualities in his character. What this definition of gentleness fails to reveal, however, is the subtle transforming power that gentleness has on our own lives as well as on the lives of those to whom we give kindness.

Demonstrating gentleness

In order for kindness to be manifest in our lives, we must become involved in the lives of other people. Gentleness needs a neighbor. Like the other aspects of the fruit of the Spirit, it is not ornamental but practical. Fruit exists to be shared and enjoyed by others. For that reason gentleness and kindness need a neighbor. In fact, I am convinced that gentleness cannot exist without a neighbor, for it can find no real expression without someone upon whom to lavish its caring. As we show kindness to others, its power is working quietly in us to free us from unhealthy preoccupation with ourselves. That involvement not only blesses the people we touch, but also acts as a wonderful door of freedom for us from unhealthy self-centered involvement.

Gentleness in confrontation

God's people bring glory to Him when they manifest gracious kindness to others. We all find some situations where it is easy to show kindness. Most of us are not so hard-hearted that we cannot be moved by a person's distress, and we will try to find a way to minister love to them in their painful situation. Yet kindness is not only to be shown to people in distress;

kindness is also love dealing with others in confronting their faults.

Perhaps nothing more frequently discredits one's testimony and ministry than showing unkindness in dealing with people. No conceivable circumstance can possibly justify a Christian's unkind treatment of others. No matter how firm we have to be in our correction and reproof, we never have an excuse to be unkind. There is no greater mark of nobility of character than the ability to reprove and correct in kindness. In Paul's "love chapter" he writes, "Love suffers long and is kind" (1 Cor. 13:4). This is a beautiful picture of the fruit of gentleness at its best, after it has "suffered" a person who has been difficult. It is a most important trait to be cultivated in preparation for working with other people.

Jesus is gentleness personified.

> Now I, Paul, who am lowly in presence among you but bold toward you while absent, appeal to you by the meekness and gentleness of Christ.
>
> —2 CORINTHIANS 10:1

Gentleness not only helps us relate to others; it also interprets Jesus for us. Jesus is gentleness. We may not understand many things about Jesus, but we do understand His kindness because we experience it every day. Gentleness is a tangible manifestation of Jesus's love and is the avenue through which His love finds expression. Jesus is not a distant, benevolent deity. He is our Savior and our friend who provides for our personal needs.

Paul also tells us that we are God's workmanship, created in Christ Jesus unto good works (Eph. 2:10). These good works become God's outlet for our kindness. Cultivating gentleness involves a conscious decision *to value the other person more highly than we value ourselves.* True kindness is not demonstrated on an occasional special event such as a holiday fruit basket. It shouldn't be confused with "voluntarianism." Being a volunteer is a vehicle through which we can transmit kindness to others. But true kindness is an integral part of the Christian character that is to be demonstrated in all our daily activities.

Those "small" kindnesses of a smile, a caring word, a listening ear, a touch of the arm, a note of encouragement, an act of including someone who feels left out, or simply being there when we are needed, are of great value. Especially to those closest to us—our mates—the fruit of gentleness needs to be displayed. We need to remember that when we speak harshly to our Christian mates, we are speaking to Christ in that tone because He lives in them. So when we speak sharply, we are mistreating Christ with our lack of kindness. There are many opportunities in the home to demonstrate the gentleness of God that will make our homes tender places of caring—a refuge from the unlovingness of the world.

Gentleness protects and affirms the dignity of the other person. How important it is to cultivate the fruit of gentleness in our lives, not only to nurture our families, but also to affirm everyone we meet. God expects us to be kind to those who are different from us, even those whom we may dislike. Sometimes disagreeable people are the ones who need our compassion more than anyone else, and often they may be the least able to return our kindness. Jesus taught us to love even our enemies (Luke 6:35). We should pray daily that God will allow people to cross our paths and give us the opportunity to reveal Jesus through kindness. Without the continual practice of showing kindness to others, we will inevitably lapse back into our self-centered ways.

Gentleness doesn't require us to become heroes, though simple acts of kindness can have such a profound impact on others as to evoke their admiration. Believers who have developed the fruit of gentleness have learned to affirm and love one person at a time. They see love where others see hatred; forgiveness where others see offenses; reconciliation where others see separation; acceptance where others see rejection; hope where others see despair; and life where others see death.

A study suggests that people who regularly help others live longer and feel better than those who are concerned only about themselves. As we have mentioned, we will discover that showing kindness is good for us as well as for those to whom we are kind. As the people of God, we are instructed to put on "a spirit of mercy, kindness, humbleness of mind, meekness, and longsuffering" (Col. 3:12). May we be those people who evidence that they have been chosen of God to be clothed with compassion and with gentleness.

Chapter 8

The Fruit of the Spirit

Part III:
Divine Goodness, Faith, Meekness, and Temperance

. . . .

Now He who supplies seed to the sower and supplies bread for your food will also multiply your seed sown and increase the fruits of your righteousness.

—2 Corinthians 9:10

. . . .

Goodness

For the fruit of the Spirit is in all goodness and righteousness and truth.

—Ephesians 5:9

Goodness can be defined as the state of being virtuous, benevolent, generous, upright, and righteous. The root word for goodness is God. So the fruit of goodness is Godlikeness demonstrated in works or acts shown to others. As it so closely relates to gentleness and kindness, it is a very practical expression or outworking of love. If man is truly good at heart, he does good to others. Those who show God's goodness will

146

be motivated by a compassion that does not change even in the face of controversy. Goodness is the Christlike nature of Godlikeness that is manifest in our lives by the power of the Holy Spirit.

How do we become like God? The only way to show forth the character of God in our lives is first to partake of His divine nature. Peter understood this when he wrote to the saints:

> His divine power has given to us all things that pertain to life and godliness through the knowledge of Him who has called us by His own glory and excellence, by which He has given to us exceedingly great and precious promises, so that through these things you might become partakers of the divine nature and escape the corruption that is in the world through lust.
>
> —2 Peter 1:3–4

God has given us everything we need through His divine power to live a godly life. When we are born again, the Holy Spirit "lifes" us with the life of Christ in order that through faith in God's promises, we can have His divine nature developed in us.

A mode of conduct

Although true goodness is a quality of divine character in our hearts wrought by the Holy Spirit, it is more than that in its expression. The term *goodness* is not simply a symbol for God, but it is a mode of conduct that becomes a way of life expressing itself in action. We might say that goodness is a habit of doing the "right" thing as defined by the Scriptures. As God's ambassadors on earth, we are to manifest God's goodness to this world (2 Cor. 5:20).

The Scriptures teach us that it is the goodness of God

147

that leads people to repentance (Rom. 2:4). It is wonderful to think that the goodness we show to people can be God's way of bringing them to repentance. When God's righteousness is manifested in our actions to people, men and women will come to God and become partakers of His divine nature themselves. That is why our Lord Jesus commands to "do good to those who hate you, and pray for those who spitefully use you and persecute you, that you may be sons of your Father who is in heaven" (Matt. 5:44–45).

Doing good to someone who does not treat you well is the zenith of benevolence; it is not the "normal" behavior for the non-Christian. A non-Christian's mode of conduct would be more like this: "Don't have anything to do with them because of the way they treated you," or "Find a way to get even with that one who hurt you." Our returning goodness to those who are unkind to us catches the world's attention because it is totally contrary to their self-centered mentality. Jesus taught us to express God's goodness in our actions toward our enemies. That vertex of goodness becomes the power of God that will lead our persecutors to repentance. In that way the world will know the power of God's love as it is displayed through human vessels.

Pharisaical goodness

There is a pharisaical, self-righteous goodness that is more of a blight to Christianity than a recommendation. Selfish goodness can be a kind of "badness" that is heaping good acts upon someone out of selfish motives to gain favor or other personal benefits. True goodness is love in action, heaping benefits on others, not with gritted teeth or ulterior motives, but motivated by compassionate love and caring without desire for personal gain.

The Christian does good acts because he is yielding to the power of the Holy Spirit. When the Holy Spirit permeates our lives, there is a positive outflow of goodness to all men. We might work with someone who is a troublemaker, who tries to upset our every effort, and who gossips about us behind our backs. Although that person is not treating us right, Jesus taught us to do good to those who despitefully use us, so we must find a way to bless that person. The Holy Spirit will show us what to do to show His goodness and, as we yield to Him, He will enable us to perform it.

The church I founded in Texas was located in a neighborhood of people who were not sympathetic with our beliefs. We were the first Charismatic group in their city at that time, and we had great difficulty trying to witness to those neighbors. Then one autumn a violent storm damaged many beautiful homes in our neighborhood, flooding them and leaving a mess in its wake. As president of our Bible College, I suggested to our students that we take this opportunity to show goodness to our neighbors. So our college students volunteered to help them scrape up mud, wash walls and drapes, and help clean up the mess. Those simple acts of goodness made an impact on the entire community. They became an example to our neighbors of the goodness of God manifest through our students by the power of the Holy Spirit. We heard statements such as, "We have never seen anything like it before, the way those young people worked."

We didn't yield to the temptation of being offended with our neighbors or developing a plan of retaliation because of their attitudes. Instead, we yielded to the Holy Spirit and found a way to bless those who had spoken against us. Some of our students baked pies and cakes for them, and offered to take care of sick babies. Many simple outworkings of the goodness of God through us became a way of "turning the other cheek." Our students made such an impression in that neighborhood that a news reporter covered the "story." The article printed in the newspaper reporting their acts of goodness erased the negative opinions in the community of our church and student body.

Goodness in sternness

In defining *goodness*, we stated that it is motivated by compassion and does not shrink from controversy. Sometimes doing good to others involves more than gentle acts, as when it requires opposing evil. Along with the gentle aspects of goodness, there are also stern qualities. Goodness will boldly represent what is right and true even when the truth hurts. Jesus demonstrated this stern aspect of goodness when He found the money changers in the temple and ran them out. He declared, "Is it not written, 'My house shall be called a house of prayer for all nations'? But you have made it a 'den of thieves.'" (Mark 11:17). His manifestation of divine goodness declared to all who witnessed that His house would be a house of purity, power, and prayer. After Jesus cleansed the temple of the evildoers, the blind and lame came to Him there, and He healed them.

It may be difficult for the natural mind to comprehend that Jesus's actions with the money changers was good. But when Jesus saw that what was going on in the temple was not right, He was moved with compassion to cleanse it so hurting people who came into the temple could have their needs met. After all, the purpose of the temple was not buying and selling. The temple was built to be a house of prayer for people who wanted to serve God. That godly purpose was made possible when Jesus threw out the money changers.

The priority of goodness is to identify the real needs of

others and find a way to meet those needs, even when such actions meet with opposition. As we have seen, it was not until Jesus had shown the stern side of goodness by cleansing the temple of evil that He was able to show the kindlier side of goodness by healing the sick. Today as well goodness needs to take a bold stance against what is wrong so what is right can prevail.

When we take our stand against the lottery and gambling that is introduced in our cities as a way of collecting taxes, we demonstrate the stern side of goodness. Although society tries to sell us a bill of goods, declaring that the lottery is a good idea, Christians know that gambling is disastrous to cities, so we must stand against it. Abortion, the murdering of innocent babies, is another issue that Christians must oppose. This national sin must be confronted and repented of so goodness can prevail. In many such ways the quality of sternness is manifest through the fruit of goodness.

How do we know when the gentle side or the stern side of goodness is needed? The key to that discernment must be found by walking in God's love and becoming sensitive to the Holy Spirit as He develops Godlikeness in us. As the character of God grows in us, it will indicate our mode of conduct for every life situation.

Faith

> Faithful is He who calls you, who also will do it.
> —1 Thessalonians 5:24

When Paul listed faith as part of the fruit of the Spirit, he used a Greek word for faith that can be translated *faithfulness* as well. Both translations are correct, though neither is complete in itself. The Greek word, *pistos*, involves the concepts of trustworthy, trustful, sure, and true in its meaning. To divide our thinking between faith and faithfulness would not do justice to the original meaning. Both faith and faithfulness involve utter reliance on God.

Faith, on one hand, involves learning to depend on God and to stand on His Word in every situation and circumstance. Faithfulness, on the other hand, is learning to yield to the Holy Spirit so we become dependable people. It is impossible to cultivate faithfulness without faith. And faith, which is complete reliance on God, is expressed through our faithfulness. We can think of both as a single coin with two sides. However, the key characteristic of each is dependency and reliance that leads to trust, which is developed through our personal relationship with God.

Perry Brewster describes faith and faithfulness this way: "While faith in God and His work is the basis of our relationship with Him, and the avenue through which His blessings flow into our lives, what is in view here is the faithfulness of character in conduct that such faith produces."[1] This fruit of faith is an aspect of character that must be carefully cultivated. It is a calm, constant, unchanging trust in God's goodness, His sovereignty, wisdom, power, and trustworthiness.

Faith is stability.

In its expression faith is demonstrated through stability. The fruit of faith doesn't panic or get frustrated, it doesn't lose the victory, and it never thinks of turning back and giving up. It maintains a serene, tranquil, and persistent reliance on God based on relationship with Him. The apostle Paul expressed this attitude of trust when he wrote, "We know that all things work together for good to those who love God, to those who are called according to His purpose" (Rom. 8:28). Of course, that promise is conditional, as stated, to those who love God and are committed to *His purposes*. If we meet those conditions, then no matter what happens, we know that God will cause it to work together to fulfill the *plan of God* in our lives and thus perform the destiny for which we were *ordained*.

Paul powerfully illustrates this reality in his second epistle to Timothy, which he wrote near the end of his life in the most discouraging of circumstances. Forsaken by once faithful friends, he is now an elderly man in jail, undoubtedly suffering physical pain and lack of warm clothing, awaiting trial, and facing execution. Yet this is what Paul said in that dismal situation: "For these things I suffer, but I am not ashamed, for I know whom I have believed, and am persuaded that He is able to keep that which I have committed to Him until that Day" (2 Tim. 1:12).

The key word here is *committed*, which means entrusted. To depend on God is to entrust ourselves to Him. If we know that we have put our lives without reservation into God's hands, we have committed our total selves to Him. Then we will know that whatever comes into our lives after that commitment is God working in us to will and to do of His good pleasure and eternal purpose (Phil. 2:13).

Cultivating faithfulness

To understand the other aspect of faith, that of faithfulness, we need to first lay hold of the reality that God is faithful. The fruit of faithfulness in our lives will be manifest as we let God work out His quality of faithfulness in us. We must realize that this process takes time. It doesn't just happen overnight, nor is it received by having someone lay hands on us. All fruit must be cultivated, and no fruit requires more cultivation than the fruit of faithfulness.

How do we cultivate a faithful heart? Jesus taught us that it starts with small things. He said, "He who is faithful in what is least is faithful also in much. And he who is dishonest in the least is dishonest also in much" (Luke 16:10). We reveal clearly what kind of person we are when we take charge of small and seemingly insignificant responsibilities. That's when our character is being tested. In God's Kingdom if we are not faithful in small things, how can we ever be promoted to be trusted with the "big" things?

Let's check ourselves to see how faithful we are in the small, apparently unimportant things of life. For example, do we make promises, perhaps to our children or our spouses, and then consistently break them? Sadly enough, some Christians are more faithful to keep their commitment to their employers than to their families. Do we continually arrive late for appointments? I believe that continual tardiness is an evidence of a weakness in one's character. God is never tardy. His sun never rises late or sets late. Everything for which He is responsible in this universe is punctual. We reveal His faithfulness in our punctuality.

Another area that reveals faithfulness is the way we handle our finances and how we pay our bills. Do we allow our bills to be overdue? Are we faithful in keeping up our accounts? According to Jesus, how we deal with money is the acid test of our faithfulness. He said if you have not been faithful in the use of unrighteous mammon, the biblical word for money, who will entrust the true riches to you (Luke 16:11)? Finally, perhaps, for more examples of faithfulness in "small" things, what about the way we return things we borrow? What about the books or other items that we borrow and do not return? In such seemingly unimportant matters our faithfulness is tested each day, for faithfulness must begin to be manifest in small things.

Trustfulness

We must always keep in mind that the purpose of bearing fruit is not for our own consumption but for others' enjoyment. Oh, that we would realize this! The fruit of the Spirit is not for our personal benefit, though we do benefit by becoming Christlike. Our purpose as fruit-bearing vines is to produce His fruit for those who are hungry. So these beautiful characteristics of faith show the Christian attitudes we should reflect toward the people whose lives we touch. In His commentary on Galatians Martin Luther made this wonderful statement:

> In listing faith among the fruit of the Spirit, Paul obviously does not mean faith in Christ, but faith in men. Such faith is not suspicious of people, but believes the best. Naturally the possessor of such faith will be deceived, but he lets it pass. He is ready to believe all men. Where this virtue is lacking, men are suspicious, forward, wayward, who believe nothing nor yield to anybody. No matter how well a person says or does anything, they will find fault with it. If you do not humor them, you can never please them. Such faith in people therefore, is quite necessary. What kind of life would this be if one person could not believe in another person.[2]

What a delicious fruit we have discovered in faith! May many who come to our tree find this fruit abundant in the life that Christ lives through us. As we learn to depend on God, His faithfulness will be revealed to us in fulfilling His promises to make us the kind of people who are trustworthy and dependable. We should want to be men and women who are faithful to God and faithful to one another.

MEEKNESS

> Take My yoke upon you, and learn from Me. For I am
> meek and lowly in heart, and you will find rest for your
> souls.
>
> —MATTHEW 11:29

Perhaps we should begin by stating emphatically that meekness does not indicate weakness. On the contrary, a truly meek person is one who displays great strength of character. Meekness is the gentle humility exhibited by those at peace with God, with themselves, and with their fellow men. The meek are accepting and doing the will of God. They are slow to anger and willing to bear offense. They are not boisterous, noisy, or selfishly aggressive. They are not boastful or contentious, but teachable and lowly in spirit.

This description of meekness must not be construed, however, to reflect a shy, timid, or weak person. Neither must the fruit of meekness be considered synonymous with cowardice or lack of leadership ability. The Scriptures declare that Moses was the meekest man in Israel (Num. 12:3), and he was their greatest leader. He was humble and patient, but also capable of firmness and great courage. His life proves that meekness is an essential characteristic of a true leader.

Growing up in the palace as the son of Pharaoh's daughter, Moses had all the advantages of wealth and power. Before the Lord could use Moses as the deliverer for His people, however, He had to strip him of Egyptian vantages and benefits. Then He had to allow the Holy Spirit to give him favorable time and occasions (forty years in the wilderness) for the purpose of God to be fulfilled in developing meekness in him. It was precisely that gentle humility that would qualify him for the task of becoming a deliverer for God's people. This meekest of all men displayed great courage as he confronted the powerful Pharaoh, divided the Red Sea, led several million of God's covenant people for forty years through the desert, transformed slaves into warriors, received and taught the law of God, administrated the first theocratic government, and stood alone before God to intercede for a rebellious nation.

Jesus declared in His sermon on the mount, "Blessed are the meek, for they shall inherit the earth" (Matt. 5:5). Even though Jesus described Himself as meek and lowly of heart (Matt. 11:29), no greater strength and power has ever been displayed on earth than that which He exercised in His ministry. He fearlessly proclaimed the truth in the face of religious leaders who plotted His death. He exercised authority over devils, disease, death, and the elements of nature by the power of His spoken word. He did not shrink from the agony of the cross. And He completed His mission on earth by totally defeating Satan and securing complete redemption for mankind.

William Vine makes this comment about meekness: "It must be clearly understood therefore that the meekness manifest by the Lord and commended to the believer is the fruit of power. The Lord was meek because He had the infinite resources of God at His command."[3] As we have seen, both Moses and Jesus were characterized as meek men, and both were men of great authority and strength. Their lives, by demonstration, help us to define the fruit of meekness.

Meekness defined

We have established that meekness has no resemblance to weakness. We have also seen that meekness is not simply gentleness. I have seen people be very kind, tender, and gentle when they pet their dog or hold a little child. But that doesn't make them meek. When we see someone who is obedient and submissive to another's will, we often classify him as a meek person. However, obedience can be a result of wrong motives such as legalism, bondage, or fear. It does not proceed necessarily from a meek heart. Meekness is not simply submission either, for one can submit to external codes of behavior because of "cultural" pressure and have absolutely no meekness in his heart.

How, then, should we describe meekness? In the biblical sense it is a combination of three characteristics—gentleness, obedience, and submission—expressed through a humble, unpretentious attitude. The meek person reflects a joyful *willingness* and a genuine *teachableness* in life situations, as well as an *acceptance* of the will of God, whatever it may be. Meekness, like the other fruit of the Spirit, is acquired by yielding to the working of the Holy Spirit in our lives. Though it may be manifest at times in a particular act in a specific situation, it won't appear fully grown in our lives overnight. First comes the blossom, and then the small fruit that needs time to grow, develop, and ripen. Like the other characteristics of love, meekness is only cultivated by our continual yielding to the Holy Spirit in all of life's circumstances. If we truly desire meekness in our lives, we must seek the things that cause it to grow.

Cultivating meekness

Jesus gave us clear instructions about cultivating meekness. He said, "Take My yoke upon you, and learn from Me. For I am meek and lowly in heart..." (Matt. 11:29). Jesus simply calls to us and invites us to submit to His yoke. He does not force us to come, but extends an invitation to take up His yoke and learn of Him. The picture of a yoke that harnesses oxen to walk together gives us the understanding that walking with

Jesus will give direction to our lives, and at the same time limit our independence. Taking His yoke willingly into our lives and submitting to His will marks the beginning of the development of the fruit of meekness. Sadly our natural flesh life does not want to stay in His yoke. It wants to rule. Staying in the yoke with Jesus is the secret of maturing that fruit.

Impact of meekness

Jesus was really teaching us how to have a true impact on our generation through developing meekness. I believe with all my heart that meekness will be one of the strongest weapons of the church against the enemy. Jesus said that the meek would inherit the earth (Matt. 5:5). Unless we understand the true power of meekness, it will be difficult for us to see how this strategy can work. But Jesus portrayed that power of meekness in His own life. When the enemy came to Jesus and found nothing in Him, he fled screaming. Through His gentle submission to His Father's will, Jesus changed the destiny of mankind.

The Scriptures are filled with instructions for us to walk in meekness. When the apostle Paul wrote guidelines for restoring a believer who had fallen, he insisted that those who restore someone do so in the spirit of meekness (Gal. 6:1). Teaching us how to deal with unrepentant people, he wrote that in meekness we instruct those who oppose themselves (2 Tim. 2:25).

Regarding treatment of fellow Christians, he instructs us to put on meekness (Col. 3:12). He wrote to Titus to show meekness to all men (Titus 3:2). Without the cultivation of this fruit, the true nature of Christ will not be seen through the church.

Promises to the meek

The call to meekness also is accompanied by divine promises for our personal lives: "But the meek…will delight themselves in the abundance of peace" (Ps. 37:11). Jesus said that those who learn meekness from Him would find rest for their souls (Matt. 11:29). Could the lack of peace in our families and our society be traced to the sad reality that so few Christians have found peace because the fruit of meekness has not been developed in their lives? If so, then our need for repentance is urgent. We must determine today to submit to Jesus's yoke and begin to cultivate the firstfruits of meekness in our lives. May we truly hear Him say, "Come to Me, all you who labor and are heavily burdened, and I will give you rest. Take My yoke upon you, and learn from Me. For I am meek and lowly in heart, and you will find rest for your souls" (Matt. 11:28–29). This rest that we find through cultivating meekness and learning of Him surpasses all human explanation.

TEMPERANCE

> He who is slow to anger is better than the mighty, and
> he who rules his spirit than he who takes a city.
> —PROVERBS 16:32

Temperance can be defined simply as self-control. Among the graces of the Spirit that are the fruit of abiding in Christ, none are more important than self-control. Temperance is the true kind of self-love. He who respects himself as the temple of the Holy Spirit will exercise control over his impulses and motivations. We usually think of temperance as moderation in the areas of eating and drinking. Temperance, however, is self-control over every phase of life. One who shows the fruit of temperance shows self-control over anger, carnal passion, appetites, desires for worldly pleasure, and our self-centered lives. Of course, this can only be accomplished by the power of the Holy Spirit who works in us His divine control that over-rules the self-life, our carnal nature.

The Scriptures teach that he who rules his spirit is better than he who captures a city (Prov. 16:32). Many people have not brought their "desire to rule" to the cross and are creating ungodly situations by trying to control others according to their selfish desires. Until the fruit of self-control is working in a person's character, he is not qualified to govern or take a place of authority in even one other life. In every area of delegated authority whether in the home, the church, or the workplace, the fruit of temperance needs to be manifested. What peace and harmony will result when leaders, counselors, pastors, and parents cultivate temperance. This understanding should cause godly parents to cultivate this fruit so they can rule their homes properly. It is important that every Christian allow the Holy Spirit to work self-control into his character.

To cultivate the fruit of temperance, our own appetites and desires must be submitted to the Lordship of Jesus and not allowed to rule us. Paul declared that all things were lawful for him, but not all things were expedient, or profitable, and that he would not be brought under the power of anything (1 Cor. 6:12). "'Food is for the belly, and the belly is for food,' but God will destroy both of them..." (1 Cor. 6:13). He went on to say in that verse that the body is for the Lord and the Lord for the body. With this perspective, we will respect ourselves and others too much to allow our carnal desire for power to rule our lives or the lives of others.

Summary

Samuel Chadwick makes the interesting observation that, in newspaper English, Paul's description of the fruit of the Spirit would read something like this:

> The fruit of the Spirit is an affectionate, lovable disposition, a radiant spirit, a cheerful temper, a tranquil mind, and quiet manner, forebearing patience in provoking circumstances with trying people, a sympathetic insight and tactful helpfulness, generous judgment; being sold to charity, loyal and reliable under all circumstances, humility that forgets self in the joy of others, in all things self-mastered, self-controlled, which is the final mark of perfection. In summarizing the subject of the fruit of the Spirit it is emphasized that these characteristics are not imposed upon the Christian from without. They are the result of the life of Christ within. They describe the character of Jesus Christ in the life of the believer.[4]

The wonderful mystery of "Christ in you, the hope of glory" (Col. 1:27) is revealed through fruit-bearing. That is only possible as we yield to the work of the Holy Spirit to become a true branch, receiving the vital life-giving sap from Christ Himself. Then we must submit to the dealings of the divine Husbandman, the Father Himself, who will not be satisfied without finding fruit in His vineyard. When He finds it, He will prune away any unnecessary material to ensure the increase of that fruitfulness. It is wonderful to think that the character of Christ Himself can flow through our lives as we submit to this precious work of the Holy Spirit to produce the fruit of love in us.

Lest we despair in thinking we cannot produce such

beautiful fruit as described here, we must understand that we need only come to Christ continually in submissive obedience to the Holy Spirit for this godly character to be cultivated in us. We need always remember that these beautiful facets of divine love have as their source, not our human efforts, but the life of God Himself. As we cultivate an intimate relationship with Christ, learning to abide in Him, we will become fruitful Christians.

Chapter 9

Walking in the Spirit

Part I:
Divine Purpose Fulfilled

. . . .

If we live in the Spirit, let us also walk in the Spirit.

—GALATIANS 5:25

. . . .

THE SCRIPTURES TEACH that if we walk in the Spirit, we will not fulfill the lust of the flesh (Gal. 5:16). As Christians, many of us have heard this biblical admonition all our lives. It gives us a beautiful picture of life in Christ and sounds like a simple command: walk in the Spirit. However, many Christians do not know what it means to walk in the Spirit. It remains a vague concept to many, even to ministers. Yet the Scriptures declare that we must live and walk in the Spirit, so we dare not settle for a vague understanding of what that involves. Instead, we need to search the Scriptures until we grasp the significance of what life is like when we walk in the Spirit. Only then can we expect to be victorious in our Christian lives.

A simple definition of what it means to walk in the Spirit is *to allow the Holy Spirit to do the work in us that God sent Him to do.* In order to cooperate fully with the work of the

Holy Spirit in our lives, we need to understand why God sent Him to us. Just before our Lord left this earth, He said this to His disciples:

> And I will pray the Father, and he shall give you another Comforter, that he may abide with you for ever; even the Spirit of truth; whom the world cannot receive, because it seeth him not, neither knoweth him: but ye know him; for he dwelleth with you, and shall be in you.
>
> —JOHN 14:16–17, KJV

As we have said, the Father sent the Holy Spirit to dwell in us and to fulfill God's eternal purpose through our lives. Unless we can grasp the greatness of His mission and His work in the earth, we will try to satisfy ourselves with a small portion of that eternal work. We may receive a few of His gifts, mistakenly thinking that is all there is of the Holy Spirit and His work. In that way many miss the reality of the eternal purposes of our Father being worked out in our lives.

We saw in our study of the gifts of the Spirit that spiritual gifts are not a prerequisite for walking in the Spirit. Paul taught the spiritually gifted Corinthian church that there was a more excellent way. He declared that if they did not follow that way of love, they were nothing, regardless of the impressive spiritual gifts they had (1 Cor. 13). That means that if we are not following the way of love, we are not walking in the Spirit at all, but are following the carnal ways of our flesh nature.

Although some have erred in overemphasizing the gifts of the Spirit, others have quenched the Holy Spirit dwelling inside them by not acknowledging His presence or consulting Him. Thus He is unable to do in them what God sent Him to do. They may acknowledge the work of Jesus on the cross and say He abides in them, yet the work of the Holy Spirit can still be foreign to them. As a result, they will never come to know Him intimately. For them He will remain some mysterious being whose Presence is something they must accept by faith without ever really understanding who He is or why He came. These people will never be able to allow the Holy Spirit to do what God sent Him to do because they do not know Him intimately.

Unfortunately the church today has erred, I believe, in both settling for a small part of the Holy Spirit's work and in quenching His moving among us. Sometimes we become satisfied with thinking that the Holy Spirit's work in us was merely to give us spiritual gifts. We think we are walking in the Spirit because the gifts of the Spirit are operating through us. Others ignore the Holy Spirit, choosing to follow man's program instead of the leading of the Holy Spirit.

Do we talk to the Holy Spirit as we do Jesus? Do we know Him intimately and personally? Do we acknowledge His presence daily? Every once in a while the Holy Spirit seems to nudge us and remind us that we haven't been very friendly to Him, that we haven't kept in very close touch with Him. It is as though He is crying out, "Don't keep Me locked up. Acknowledge that I am here. Recognize what I have come to do." The time must come that we get serious about who the Holy Spirit is and learn why He came to earth. Then we must choose to cooperate with Him and allow Him to do all that God has sent Him to do. We need to ask Him, "Why did You come?" and "Why did My Father send You to me?" Then as He answers us and reveals to us His divine purposes, we must yield to His work in our lives and churches.

Person of Purpose

The Holy Spirit is a divine Person with a plan and purpose for our lives. He doesn't come to us haphazardly; He is a Person of purpose. God has an eternal plan and purpose for every individual who accepts Him as Lord and Savior. The Holy Spirit is God bringing that purpose to reality as we learn to yield to His will for our lives. Paul declared to the Corinthians, "What? Do you not know that your body is the temple of the Holy Spirit…?" (1 Cor. 6:19) The Holy Spirit does not reside in the church building; He lives in us. Though He resides in our spirits, His work is limited by what we allow Him to do through our souls and bodies.

That is why we need to die to our soulish nature; it is so we can cooperate with Him to accomplish His purposes. Our carnal minds need to be renewed by the Spirit of God within us to think His thoughts. Our wills need to be yielded to Him to obey His will. Our emotions need to be filled with the love of God. As we begin to discuss what it means to walk in the Spirit, we need to understand the specific purposes for which God comes to dwell in us.

A place of spiritual discernment

What is His purpose when He comes into our temples to live in them? One of the first things He does is to make our hearts a place of spiritual discernment. In our study of spiritual gifts we saw that the Holy Spirit Himself living in us gives us ability to discern what spirit we are encountering in a certain situation: the Holy Spirit, an evil spirit, or the human spirit. Though all may not operate the gift of discerning of spirits, when the Holy Spirit comes into our hearts, He brings

His divine ability to discern and makes our "temples" a place of spiritual discernment.

Why do I list spiritual discernment first in considering the purposes for the coming of the Holy Spirit? Until the Holy Spirit comes to us, we are living under the influence of another spirit. Paul declared:

> And you were dead in your trespasses and sins, in which you formerly walked according to the course of this world, according to the prince of the power of the air, of the spirit that is now working in the sons of disobedience.
> —EPHESIANS 2:1–2, NAS

Before our salvation we were cooperating with the spirit of this world that is inspired by Satan. So our inner man was under the influence of that spirit. If we are going to submit to the Holy Spirit, He has to be able to teach us to discern which spirit is to abide there. We have a mind of our own, and the devil has one too. If we can't discern, we don't know who is influencing us. We need to have a place of spiritual discernment inside of us. We call it "walking softly," or "ascertaining the voice of the Spirit." He needs to set up discernment inside us so we can recognize what is good and evil, holy and profane. If we can't discern righteousness from unrighteousness, we won't be able to walk with Him. If we can't discern truth, we can't relate to the Spirit of truth. The Holy Spirit will put a caution in our minds when we hear something that is not quite right. Those checks become safeguards that keep us from error. We need to learn to listen to those impressions and then learn to test them, trying the spirits.

A place of victory over sin

He came to make us *victorious over sin*. The Scriptures teach, "For sin shall not have dominion over you" (Rom. 6:14). There is the power of sin, the pollution of sin, and the penalty for sin. God came to deliver us from all the dominion of sin. When people do not live victoriously, they are not walking in the Holy Spirit. Even if they speak in tongues as an evidence of having received the baptism of the Holy Spirit, that is not a criteria for walking in the Spirit. He came to make this temple a place of victory over sin, and having that victory means we are walking in the Spirit.

Does that mean I won't ever sin again? No. But sin does not have to control me. As I yield to the Holy Spirit, He delivers me from the sin, and I don't have to live in it. He changes my desires so I don't want to live the way I did under sin. I don't have to have people watching me to make me keep the rules. I walk obediently because the victory is dwelling in me. I don't have to be restricted to turn off immoral programs on my TV. My own desires scream against them. The Holy Spirit is controlling my desires and enabling me to hate the things God hates. So He came to give us that victory until sin no longer has dominion over us.

A place of refreshing rain

The Holy Spirit makes our hearts ready to receive the *refreshing rain* that God promises. He knows that without rain, we can't produce fruit. He knows that unless we have showers, our hearts will get hard. Have you ever seen rain fall when the ground was so hard that the water didn't soak it? That is a picture of people who come to church when the Spirit is moving, and the rain of His presence rolls off like water from a duck's back because their hearts are too hard to receive it. The rain of the Spirit brings repentance. Repentance will break the soil and the fallow ground. He comes in conviction to our temples and prepares them as places where the showers of the latter rain of refreshing can fall.

A place of healing and deliverance

The Holy Spirit has come to make our temples places of *healing*. Jesus is the Anointed One who brings healing and deliverance to captives. He acknowledged the fact that the Holy Spirit empowered Him for every good work when He stood up in church to read, "The Spirit of the Lord is upon Me, because He has anointed Me to preach the gospel to the poor; He has sent Me to heal the broken-hearted, to preach deliverance to the captives" (Luke 4:18). The good news of the gospel is for the poor. The "poor" does not refer to people who do not have material possessions, but to those who recognize their need of God. What is the first declaration of the constitution of the heavenly government? "Blessed are the poor in spirit, for theirs is the kingdom of heaven" (Matt. 5:3). The poor in spirit are those who know they have a need and who look to God for help. What is available to them? It is the Kingdom. Under this anointing, by the Spirit of the Lord, Jesus proclaims freedom to captives in bondage to sin and disease. So anytime the Holy Spirit begins to move in the church, part of the message is freedom from bondage, recovery of sight to the blind, and deliverance of the oppressed.

As we can understand from the passage in Luke 4, the healing that the Holy Spirit came to set up inside us is not limited to physical distresses. He came to bring divine help to the mind, to the will, to the emotions, to any part of us that has been injured or bruised. In whatever way we are lame or crippled—physically, mentally, or emotionally—He has come to bring divine enablement. We do not need to wallow in self-pity over our emotional hurts or use the past as an excuse for present failure. We hear the cry so often today, "I was abused." Though it is sadly true that many have suffered deeply from traumatic experiences, it is equally true that the Holy Spirit came to bring healing. If, as Christians, we haven't experienced His healing in certain areas of our lives, is it not that we haven't allowed Him to do that healing work in us? We need to find a place of forgiveness and yieldedness to His love and power that will free us from the effects of our past.

You may ask me, "Have you ever been hurt or rejected or abused?" Of course I have. "Have you ever had anybody do something to make you bitter?" Of course I have. But I did not have to succumb to bitterness and other negative strongholds, for I discovered Somebody living in me who can handle it. When I am thinking about that difficult person or circumstance, He says, "Would you like to see your healed condition inside?" And He shows me that it is as though He has dropped a glass bubble between me and the difficulty, and I can look through the glass shield without feeling any disturbance of anger, retaliation, or hurt emotions. I have been given grace to forgive and that becomes my key to the healing of my hurt. The healing of the Holy Spirit, then, is for even the deepest pain: bruisings, batterings, broken hearts. He came to make us whole, not only in our bodies, but also in our psyches and emotions as well. Though we are powerless to heal ourselves, the Holy Spirit brings our healing by His divine power.

A place of soul-winning and missionary zeal

The Holy Spirit comes to set up a zeal in our hearts for winning the lost to Christ. Jesus promised the disciples, "But you shall receive power when the Holy Spirit comes upon you. And you shall be My witnesses..." (Acts 1:8). One of the sure proofs that He has come to our hearts is "after that" we become witnesses. Where do we begin to be witnesses? Jesus said we begin in our Jerusalem, the place where we live—home base.

Your world is where you personally touch lives. As you experience this zeal and power to witness to your world, it is an evidence that the Holy Spirit has come. It is the Holy Spirit's business to win the world to Jesus. Jesus commissioned His disciples to go to all the world. A Spirit-led life will have that mandate. A Spirit-led church has the same mandate to go into all the world with the gospel. Where the Holy Spirit is working, He is working to bring souls of men to Jesus.

A place where strongholds of Satan are conquered

Is conquering strongholds different from gaining victory over sin? Yes. It is even greater than gaining victory over sin. I know that some say the church is not to be militant, that we are to be lovers of the Lamb, cultivating relationship with our heavenly Bridegroom. I agree with them that we are to be in love with Jesus, but I disagree with the extreme of saying we are never to be involved in spiritual warfare. God gave the church the power over Satan. He deputized us, equipped us, and sent us out with authority over devils and diseases. The church is learning both to worship the Lamb and to do warfare—not by our power, but by the power of the Spirit. It is God pulling down strongholds, but He has to do it through the church. If we can stand against the enemy with vessels that are clean and release the Holy Ghost in us, He will pull down the strongholds of the enemy.

In the 1500s the queen of England said she feared the prayers of John Knox more than the whole enemy's army. He was a man of God who knew God's power over the enemy. What does the enemy think of us? The church is not a weak, passive, defeated group of people. The church is the body of Christ anointed by the power of the Holy Ghost to preach the gospel to the poor, to set the captives free, and to tear down strongholds. The Holy Spirit gives us authority to take back what the devil stole.

A place where backsliding can be removed

The Holy Spirit comes into our lives to bring restoration to our souls. Everything the enemy has perpetrated against the human race, God has purposed to restore. Jesus came to undo, outdo, and overdo everything the devil ever did. The Holy Spirit is restoring us to relationship with God the Father and God the Son, teaching us to walk with Him in obedience and to enjoy the kingdom of God in righteousness, peace, and joy in the Holy Ghost.

These are the wonderful purposes of the Holy Spirit in coming to redeem a life from the power of sin. How does He come to fulfill these purposes? What must we do to enjoy the benefits of His coming? The first requirement for having the purposes of God revealed in us is we must be born again of the Spirit of God. There is more involved in this experience than simply signing a paper to join a church. Understanding what actually takes place when we are born of the Spirit will prepare us to receive all the fullness of God's purposes for our lives. Though I had been saved many years when the Holy Spirit began to teach me about the new birth, I realized I had not understood very well what was involved in this experience.

BORN OF THE SPIRIT

Sons of God are described in the Scriptures as those who are led by the Spirit (Rom. 8:14). The Bible has much to say about our three developmental stages of walking with God: baby-hood, youth, and adulthood. There is a vast difference between being a baby born into a family and being a son who has come to maturity. Sonship in the Scriptures indicates a mature rela-tionship with the Father, involving both privilege and responsi-bility. God wants not only sons, but also sons with knowledge. Sons with knowledge are those who walk in revelation and who know what their Father is thinking. There are some grown children who can't "run the company." The spiritual son with knowledge is the one who has been trained in the ways of the Father so that he can reign with Him.

The first requirement for becoming a mature son of God is that we must be *born of the Spirit*. What does it mean to be born of the Spirit? Nicodemus asked Jesus, "How can a man be born when he is old? Can he enter a second time into his mother's womb and be born?" (John 3:4) Jesus told Nicodemus that unless he was born again, he could not see the kingdom of God. Do we really know what He meant? As evangelicals, we have taught people that they must be born again to get to heaven. That was all we offered in our understanding of salva-tion. We knew that one day we would die, and that in order to go to heaven we must be born again. That is true, but that is not all God intended in offering us eternal life through the new birth.

We live in a world where there are two kingdoms. One is the satanic kingdom of darkness and of lies. The other is the kingdom of light, love, and truth—the kingdom of God. Those who live in sin are being controlled by a satanic power that rules that kingdom. Though they might be considered moral, pay their bills, and choose a decent lifestyle, they are living in the kingdom of darkness that is opposed to the kingdom of God. When Jesus walked this earth, He said, "The kingdom of heaven is at hand" (Matt. 4:17). His kingdom has come for those who are willing to receive it through repentance. Asking Jesus to forgive our sins and to be Lord of our lives, and acknowledging His sacrifice on Calvary, brings the kingdom of God to us and ushers us into that kingdom here on the earth.

Entering the kingdom of God through the new birth means our inner man has entered into eternity now. When we are born of the Spirit, we are alive to the eternal realities of the kingdom of God. I am not simply going into eternity when I die. My spirit is already living in the eternal kingdom of God as a born-again child of God. I can't see the kingdom of God unless I am born of the Spirit, taught by the Spirit, and led by the Spirit because it is a spiritual kingdom. Jesus said, "That which is born of the flesh is flesh, and that which is born of the Spirit is spirit" (John 3:6). To be born of the Spirit means to be born from above, to receive a new spiritual life of divine origin.

I had preached the gospel for seventeen years when I was miraculously healed from what was believed to be a terminal illness. I received the baptism of the Holy Spirit at the same time, and both experiences were against my theology at that time. A little while after that my heavenly Father talked to me about what actually happened when I was born again. I was a little insulted because I thought I had come into revelation of much deeper things than the new birth. I thought I understood the new-birth experience.

The Holy Spirit gave me a vision of a Jewish girl, a little maiden in a kneeling position. I knew it was Mary, the mother of Jesus. She was enveloped in the Shekinah glory of God.

I saw a beautiful cloud around her as He let me look in on that scene. Then He asked me, "What happened to her that brought your Savior to the earth?" I answered simply, "She became pregnant." He responded, "What produced that child?" I said, "A seed." Then He asked, "Whose seed?" I answered, "God's." He continued His questions to me as a patient teacher: "Where did I put that seed?" I responded, "In Mary's uterus." Then He asked me what her response was. I replied, "She said, 'Be it unto me according to Thy Word.'" She was saying, in essence, "Let me become pregnant according to your Word." The Father explained, "From My mind, I produced from Myself a Seed, the Word." When He said that, I remembered how John began his Gospel: "In the beginning was the Word, and the Word was with God, and the Word was God....And the Word was made flesh, and dwelt among us..." (John 1:1, 14, KJV). Then He asked me, "Who took that seed from God to Mary?" I said, "The Holy Spirit." Then He made me understand that in that same supernatural way, when I was born again, the Holy Spirit planted the seed of God's eternal life in my spirit through His Word. That is how Christ comes to live in my spirit.

Paul called this experience a mystery: "this mystery among the nations. It is Christ in you, the hope of glory" (Col. 1:27). A number of times in the Christological epistles he talks about our being "in Christ" and Christ being "in us." After the Holy Spirit visited Mary and impregnated her with the seed of God, Mary extolled the greatness of God in her lovely "Magnificat": "My soul magnifies the Lord" (Luke 1:46). She was expressing the wonder of that divine life within her. In that same way, there is a new creation living inside of us, in our spirits. "Therefore, if any man is in Christ, he is a new creature" (2 Cor. 5:17). Who is this new creature inside us? It is Christ.

We are new in that we are born from above, and our eternal spirits are now alive to God. He is eternal life. If we have Jesus, we have eternal life; if we do not have Christ, we do not have eternal life.

The Holy Spirit hovered over us, just as He did over the earth when it was without form and void, and created new life in us. He said, in effect, "Let there be light, life, love, liberty"—and He lifed us with eternal life. Without that supernatural spiritual birth, we cannot even see the kingdom of God. These human eyes can never see the kingdom of God. That is the reason we don't look for God in miracles. Miracles do not reveal Jesus; they show you where Jesus has been. Everywhere He went, He did good. Miracles help the natural man to see that there is a God, but we don't have to have them to see God.

Paul told the Corinthians, "'Eye has not seen, nor ear heard, nor has it entered into the heart of man the things which God has prepared for those who love Him.' But God has revealed them to us by His Spirit" (1 Cor. 2:9–10). He understood that only by the Spirit of God can we know the mind and purpose of God for us. Why are we disturbed when unsaved people can't understand what we Christians do about worship and praise, for example? It is not possible for the natural man to be able to comprehend and see what is in the kingdom of God. Why? The kingdom is a spirit world ruled by King Jesus and administrated by the Holy Spirit. He is the executor, divine administrator, and the teacher. He came to make the kingdom real to us and to put us into the kingdom. We are citizens of another world. Without experiencing a supernatural new birth by the Spirit of God, a person cannot enjoy this wonderful kingdom, a kingdom of peace, joy, and righteousness in the Holy Ghost (Rom. 14:17).

I have a King in me now who has started to reign and

rule in the eternal part of my inner man. One day He will be released to be King over all. Even as Christians, having experienced the new birth, we must be careful to focus our minds and hearts on the eternal kingdom. Although we must live and work in this world, we dare not set our affections and pursuits on the values of this world system. The more we crave what is here, and the more the system of this world takes hold of us, the less we will know about the kingdom of God. If we expect to grow from babyhood to youth and into sons with knowledge, we will have to concentrate our energies on the pursuit of God and His holiness and righteousness in every area of our lives.

Our Dilemma

> Therefore, if any man is in Christ, he is a new creature. Old things have passed away. Look, all things have become new.
> —2 Corinthians 5:17

If we do not understand what it means to be born again and become a new creature in Christ, we will be disappointed and discouraged in our walk when we discover that some of the old things of our lives still seem to be very present. The anger that ruled us before salvation may continue to plague us at times, though we do not want to give place to it. If we dogmatically declare that we are new creatures and that old things are passed away, but our behavior and attitudes do not show it, it is because we haven't understood what is really involved in this experience.

A translation of this verse that is closer to the original Greek would be, "Therefore if any man be *in Christ a new creature*, old things are continually passing away." This shows the progressive work of salvation in our souls. We must learn to allow the Christ-life in our spirits to permeate our soulish natures—our wills, minds, and emotions—by yielding to the Holy Spirit within us instead of to our sin nature. We still have our soulish nature to bring to the cross of Christ, surrendering its evil deeds to the Lordship of Christ. We are in Christ and He is in us, so all things are becoming new as the old are passing away. We have Someone new living in us as the pregnant mother has the new creature inside her. Christ's life was breathed into us when we asked Him to save us from our sins, and He took the Word and made it alive, planting His life inside us. As we yield to His wonderful divine life, we can be changed into His likeness.

We can be delivered from our dilemma as Paul so graphically describes it to the Romans:

> For I joyfully concur with the law of God in the inner man, but I see a different law in the members of my body, waging war against the law of my mind....Wretched man that I am! Who will set me free from the body of this death? Thanks be to God through Jesus Christ our Lord!
>
> —ROMANS 7:22–25, NAS

As we yield to the life of Christ in our spirits, we can overcome our nature that is given to sin and grow into Christlikeness to become mature sons. We have to give up our lives in order to receive His. To the degree that we exchange our old nature at the cross, choosing to die to its sinful ways, we receive His life. John the Baptist understood this principle when he declared, "He must increase, but I must decrease" (John 3:30).

Paul declared, "I have been crucified with Christ. It is no

longer I who live, but Christ who lives in me. And the life I now live in the flesh, I live by faith in the Son of God, who loved me and gave Himself for me" (Gal. 2:20). So as that new life comes forth, the life I now live, I live by *the faith of the Son of God*. Judicially I am crucified with Christ; the death of my sin nature has been legally accomplished. It was nailed to the cross on which Jesus died. My old Adamic, sinful, ungodly nature is reckoned dead, powerless to rule me any longer, as I bring it to the cross and refuse to yield to its ways. We are powerless to change ourselves, but as we allow the Holy Spirit to birth the life of Christ within us, we can continually yield to Him and be changed into the image of Christ.

If I am in Christ, I am a new creature. I don't even have to rely on my faith to experience that reality. For a long time the devil told me I didn't have any faith, until one day I was able to refute him with the Word. Faith is a gift of God, not something we work up ourselves. Paul taught, "For by grace you have been saved through faith, and this is not of yourselves. It is the gift of God" (Eph. 2:8). Now I say as Paul did, "The life which I now live in the flesh I live by *the faith of the Son of God*, who loved me, and gave Himself for me" (Gal. 2:20, KJV, emphasis added).

We are saved by grace through faith. It is not ours; it is His. It is His grace, His faith, His wisdom, His knowledge, and His holiness. The beautiful thing is, when we go into business with Him, He furnishes all the capital. We don't have much to invest. Whose grace is working? Whose mercy? Whose wisdom? Whose righteousness? We don't have much to boast about except the new Person who is living inside us. He does not take us over and possess us as a demon spirit does. But to the degree that we give Him our wills, He gives us His will in exchange. To the degree we give up our carnal minds and opinions, He gives us His mind. He uses our minds, He doesn't destroy them. As we yield our carnal minds to Him, He gives us the mind of Christ. And to the degree we yield our emotions to Him, He fills us with His joy and peace.

The development of the Christ-life within us is so beautiful! We have been breathed upon by the Holy Spirit as Mary was, and this holy thing within us is Jesus. We can call it "eternal life" or "Christ" or "glory." It is He! In our born-again experience He has moved in to give us what we don't have and to furnish everything we will need to live our lives in Christ. The more we let the life of Christ grow, the more His divine nature becomes our nature. We begin to realize that we don't get angry like we used to, for Christ doesn't react like that. We begin to love people we could not love before. We are delivered from fear because "perfect love casts out fear" (1 John 4:18). All of our sin nature loses its power over us as we allow the life of Christ to mature us into responsible sons and daughters of God.

As we begin to understand the work of the Holy Spirit in salvation, we can learn to yield to Him in such a way that we will fulfill the requirements for walking in the Spirit and receive the blessings that are a result of living a Spirit-filled life.

Chapter 10

Walking in the Spirit

Part II:
Divine Requirements and Blessings

. . . .

I say then, walk in the Spirit, and you
shall not fulfill the lust of the flesh.

—GALATIANS 5:16

. . . .

As WE EXPLORE the divine requirements and inevitable results of walking in the Spirit, we can evaluate whether or not we are living a life that is fulfilling the biblical mandate to walk in the Spirit and not fulfill the lust of the flesh. God's truths are not difficult to understand when the Holy Spirit gives revelation to our hearts. But He always waits for us to choose His way. He will never violate our wills in the matters of relationship, even though He knows we will suffer loss if we do not obey His commands. In the Scriptures God has given us many beautiful examples of people who followed Him in obedience and of the blessing that came to their lives as a result. We see this in a beautiful love story in the Book of Genesis, which typifies our relationship with the Holy Spirit.

The Holy Spirit Typified in Genesis

In the story of Abraham sending his servant, Eliezer, to look for a bride for his son, Isaac (Gen. 24), we find a beautiful revelation of the Holy Spirit. This Old Testament type shows us the relationship between the believer and the Holy Spirit, as well as the relationship of the Godhead. Eliezer, a type of the Holy Spirit, is the faithful servant who leaves the father's house to go to a far country and seek a bride for the son. The drama begins with this journey of the servant from the father's house and ends in his triumphant return with a bride of Isaac, the son. Eliezer made a covenant with the father, Abraham, to bring back a bride for his son. As surely as this servant returned with Rebekah to present her as the bride for Isaac, so shall the Holy Spirit return to the heavenly Father with a bride for our Lord Jesus Christ. What actually happened in Rebekah's life should be of great interest to every believer who desires to be a part of that bride.

The name *Eliezer* means a "mighty divine helper." This faithful servant's entire mission and purpose focused on one thing: to fulfill the father's desire for a bride for his son. He realized he would have to get the girl to choose to leave behind her family, friends, home, and all she had. His commission was that she become enamored with Isaac, as well as espoused or engaged to him. As Christians, we have been chosen to be the bride of Christ. The Holy Spirit has come to be our "mighty helper" to help us become that spotless bride. We must understand, however, that bride-ship is not an *appointment*; it is a *relationship* of choice. To me that statement unlocks the entire mystery of who is going to be a part of the bride.

We will become the bride of Christ in eternity because of our love relationship with our Lord here on the earth. If

He is truly our Bridegroom by choice of relationship, and we have a passion for Him, He will one day be our Bridegroom. The heavenly Father sent the Holy Spirit to bring us into this love relationship with Jesus. As we learn to trust Him, He will woo us, win us, teach us, lead us, and bring us safely home as Christ's eternal bride.

As Eliezer began his search for a bride for Isaac, he prayed for God to help him find the right girl. He asked that she would be at the well drawing water at evening time, and that she would offer to give him water and to water his camels as well. We can easily understand the application of this type as we are admonished in the Scriptures to draw water from the wells of salvation and to become servants of all. It was Rebekah who displayed this servant's heart, and Eliezer knew she was the answer to his prayer.

He then gave Rebekah many gifts: gold bracelets, earrings, jewels, and silver. Eliezer received those gifts from the father before he left home. The father sent them for the bride and wanted the servant to give them to her along the journey so they might give her a little understanding of the generous nature of her bridegroom. In that same way, the Holy Spirit gives us spiritual gifts to reveal our Bridegroom to us and show us the benevolent heart and kindness of the Father.

The purpose of the gifts, however, was not that Rebekah became satisfied with them alone. She could have stayed in her home with her new gifts, delighting in the fact that she had been chosen to become a bride. These gifts did not obligate her to choose to leave her home. But to become the bride of Isaac, she had to choose to be chosen. That choice would require her leaving all that was familiar and taking an arduous journey by camel across the desert to be united with her bridegroom. As we know, Rebekah made that choice and became the bride of Isaac.

The Holy Spirit is our divine Eliezer whom we must choose to follow as Rebekah did this earthly servant. Learning to walk in the Spirit will require following the Holy Spirit in obedience wherever He leads us. Just as Eliezer was successful in bringing home a bride for Isaac, the Holy Spirit will also be successful in finding those who will choose to follow Him to their heavenly Bridegroom.

In contrast to Rebekah's obedience we can observe the disobedience of the children of Israel who were also chosen of God to be a special nation. A whole generation who had known the miraculous gifts of God never followed Him into the Promised Land. They were stubborn and rebellious, living in spiritual adultery. Yes, they were chosen by God, but they had never chosen to separate themselves unto their God and be cleansed of their unbelief so they could fulfill His purposes. So when it was time to go into Canaan, God could not take them into it. It was as though they had learned nothing of God during their forty years in the wilderness. They were still self-centered, seeking only for the provision that God had given them without loving and trusting the Person of God Himself.

This is a sad picture of so many Christians today who have received the gifts of the Holy Spirit, but who have not allowed the Holy Spirit to lead them into holiness of life, into the character of Christ. They have gloated over being chosen and called of God. However, they have not wanted the discipline of separation that Rebekah chose, or the rigorous "camel" journey that would prepare them for meeting the bridegroom. Instead, they want to rebuke the testings that have been sent to work in them the character of holiness. If we shoot our camels, how will we make the journey home to see our Bridegroom? Those lumbering beasts of trials and tests, as uncomfortable as they may be, are the only vehicle that we have been given to get us to our destination.

Do we see ourselves in the story of Rebekah as humble servants choosing to follow our divine Helper? Or do we fit easier into the story of the grumbling, unbelieving Israelites? If we see ourselves in the latter, we need to ask the questions, "Do I love the Lord Jesus with all my heart? Is He the lover of my soul? Is my passion for Him growing and consuming me more day by day?" Rebekah was asked the question, "Wilt thou go with this man?" What would our answer be to leaving all and following the Lord? Rebekah made her choice to follow the servant and become the bride of Isaac.

If we read the story of Eliezer carefully, we understand that this servant had focused on this one ultimate intention and purpose: to please his master by bringing home a bride for his son. The entire work of the Holy Spirit is related to His divine purpose of bringing home the bride of Christ. He didn't come simply to help us cope with life or to bless us with spiritual gifts.

Our Comforter

Although it is true that the Holy Spirit became our divine Comforter, that is not His ultimate purpose in our lives. Every manifestation of Himself, every divine touch we feel on our lives, is intended to reveal Christ to us and in us, preparing us to meet our Bridegroom. Neither did He come simply to give spiritual gifts to the church. Every gift has a purpose.

If He wants you to prophesy, your prophecy is to glorify Christ. If He lets you speak in divers tongues, it is so a person in that language may hear of the glorious works of our Lord. In everything He does He is saying, in effect, "Behold Jesus.

Consider Jesus. Isn't He wonderful? He is the Alpha and the Omega, the Beginning and the End. He is the Healer. He is the Revelation of the Father." The Holy Spirit came to reveal Jesus to us so we can fall passionately in love with Him and be prepared to be His bride.

Jesus said, "When the Counselor comes, whom I shall send to you from the Father...He will bear witness of Me" (John 15:26). The Holy Spirit's prime message is Jesus. He came to serve Jesus, to reveal Jesus, to quicken our lives with the life of Jesus in and through us. We need to remember that we are not our own; we have been bought with a price. We have been chosen to be espoused to Christ. The Holy Spirit came to guide us into all truth, and the truth will set us free from every bondage to sin and unbelief. We are not of this world. We are on a journey toward a glorious meeting with our Bridegroom. We are being prepared for the presentation of the bride and the coronation of the queen.

Our guide

We often hear believers say that the Holy Spirit "led them" into something they desire to do, and many cry out for Him to give direction when they are in trouble. Yet, many times when He is trying to lead us, we don't yield to His guidance. We spend time trying to decide what to do for ourselves and figuring out how we can do it. Somehow we cannot quite comprehend that the third Person of the infinite Godhead lives inside us, whose eternal purpose is to fulfill the eternal plan of our Father in us. If we yield to Him and walk in His love, we will not fulfill the lust of the flesh. Why? The Holy Spirit is continually showing us Jesus in all His beauty, the beauty of holiness. He is enamoring our hearts with Christ and changing us from our selfish desires to an all-consuming desire to please Him alone.

It seems to me that in these days the Holy Spirit is opening the eyes of His chosen ones and answering the prayer Paul prayed for the Ephesians:

> That the God of our Lord Jesus Christ, the Father of glory, may give you the Spirit of wisdom and revelation in the knowledge of Him, that the eyes of your understanding may be enlightened, that you may know what is the hope of His calling and what are the riches of the glory of His inheritance among the saints.
>
> —EPHESIANS 1:17–18

When the Holy Spirit prayed this prayer through Paul, He was praying the will of God for the church today as well as for the Ephesian church. Paul addressed his epistle not only to the church at Ephesus, but also to the faithful in Christ Jesus. That includes everyone who loves Christ. The Holy Spirit will be faithful to open the eyes of every church that wants His presence and is praying this kind of prayer. This revelation comes to believers who have no concern other than to see the body of Christ conformed to the image of our Lord Jesus Christ. We have had the era of a "word of wisdom" and a "word of knowledge," but the Holy Spirit is praying that we might have the Spirit of wisdom and the *Spirit* of knowledge and revelation.

The bride

The Holy Spirit's mission will be complete only when He does what He promised the Father He would do: bring back the bride for the Son. What kind of bride do you think He is going to present to the Father on the day when our Lord is finally revealed in His ultimate glory? Will He choose her from among those who live with a Sunday morning mentality, who are filled with apathy and love for material things, and who worship as a religious duty once a week? Or will she be among those who are not devoted to Jesus and haven't cared about an intimate relationship with the Lord—those who are not truly in love with Him? I don't think that is the kind of bride He is going to present to Jesus.

The bride of Christ will include those who are willing to "ride the camels" that represent those painful trials in our lives. Rebekah chose that long, tedious camel ride through the hot desert, following her guide, enduring the bumps and dust, and being willing to leave her personal comforts of home. She set her eyes on reaching her destiny. If we truly love Jesus, we will be found following the Holy Spirit wherever He leads us, despite our personal discomfort because we have chosen to leave all to find our Bridegroom.

The bride of Christ will have the yearning of the heart that says, as did David Wilkerson, "Jesus, You are the only happiness in this world. I have tasted and seen that You are good. And all I want is You." This is the deep inner cry of those who hunger for holiness. They suddenly begin to feel a deep remorse and anguish over their sins and iniquity that are revealed to them by the Holy Spirit. When they begin to pray, the Holy Spirit Himself comes to help their infirmities and to pray according to the will of God for them (Rom. 8:26–27). He is praying with such profound emotion that it becomes "groanings which cannot be uttered." He intercedes for the perfect will of the Father—the purpose over our lives that was ordained before the foundation of the world to be fulfilled in us. Our hearts long for Christ. This Holy Spirit-breathed "longing" is a powerful experience, and He groans in us because He knows the will of God is not yet accomplished. We begin to realize how far He has yet to take us before we are transformed into the image of Christ and evidence His character in our lives.

Where are those today who are experiencing this yearning and groaning to be more like Christ, with a thirst for righteousness and a passion for God? Many churches seem to be filled with people who never evaluate their love for Christ. They don't want to be disturbed. But the Holy Spirit is finding people who are allowing Him to take control of their lives. There is a "church within the church" of believers who are learning to hear the voice of the Holy Spirit and are beginning to yield to Him.

The more they yield, the more His inner groaning comes forth. They are praying in agreement with the Holy Spirit. Their cry is, "Holy Spirit, do what the Father sent You to do. Whatever it takes, reveal Christ in my heart so I may be totally weaned from this world." They are allowing the Holy Spirit to convict them of sin and cleanse them so they can live holy lives. They are learning to walk in the Spirit so they will not fulfill the lust of the flesh.

If this is your testimony, you can rejoice. The Holy Spirit wants you to be cleansed from every spot and wrinkle to fulfill His ultimate purpose to bring home to the Father a spotless bride for His Son. If you walk in the Spirit, you will be yielding in obedience to His leading. If you let Him do His cleansing work in you, allowing Him to fulfill the Father's eternal purpose, you will know what it means to walk in the Spirit.

Requirements for Walking in the Spirit

Dependence

As we observe Rebekah's choice to follow the servant, we can see that she was completely *dependent* on him for her future. In that same way, we are dependent on the Holy Spirit. Not only does He save us and give us spiritual gifts, but He is also responsible for our entire well-being: spirit, soul, and body. We are completely dependent on Him, whether or not we consciously feel His presence. All believers know what it is at times to enjoy the conscious presence of the Holy Spirit. When I was first filled with the Spirit, I thought I was always going to feel His presence and be aware of Him.

Then one day when I was distressed because I did not feel His nearness, He gave me a beautiful object lesson. He said to me, "You loved your daddy dearly." That is true. He continued, "When you went to bed and said good-night to your daddy, did he have to stay in the room all night to prove to you he was there? Did he have to wake you up every few minutes and say, 'Daughter, I am here'? Or did you go to sleep trusting him, knowing that he was there, and if the slightest disturbance came, you would be conscious of his presence?" I understood then that I did not always have to have a consciousness of the presence of the Holy Spirit with me. I needed only to trust Him with my life as I had trusted my earthly daddy unreservedly as a child.

Our dependence upon the Holy Spirit becomes a life force, like it did in Jesus's life (John 5:30). Andrew Murray defines humility as "the place of entire dependence on God."[1] We must humble ourselves to recognize the Holy Spirit as the One who quickens our lives. We must depend on Him not only for our spiritual life, but also for the needs of our souls: our minds, wills, and emotions. To be totally dependent on Him doesn't make us puppets. It simply means that we have chosen to yield our wills to the Holy Spirit who furnishes the ability to do what we could not have done without Him. Instead of relying on our natural minds, we learn to consult our divine guide and teacher.

How I learned a new dependence on the Holy Spirit

The Holy Spirit required total dependence of me at a critical time in my life. At the same time that I was healed from a terminal illness, I received the baptism of the Holy Spirit. I discovered that the third Person of the Godhead had come to live in me. Though I had thought He had been in control of this body during seventeen years I had been in the ministry, I was mistaken. I thought I had known Him in His fullness as a minister and college professor in the old-time Methodist faith, struggling to live a victorious life over my sin nature. When I would miss the mark, I would come under condemnation because of the legalism I had embraced. Then when I was gloriously healed and baptized in the Holy Spirit, I became very aware that a divine Person, whom I knew very little about, had come to take up His residence inside me. I had preached about Him in theory and had preached that He sanctified us because that was what I was taught. Now I felt the presence of a divine Person and heard Him speak inside me.

At that same time, to my dismay the Scriptures seemed to become meaningless to me. I would read my Bible, but it was like a blank book. I couldn't even recall what I had preached all those years. For the next few months the Holy Spirit gave me only four verses of Scripture to sustain me. They became life to me in a new dimension. The first one was from the Book of Proverbs: "Trust in the LORD with all your heart; and lean not on your own understanding" (Prov. 3:5). The Holy Spirit was cleansing my mind of the way I had always understood the Scriptures. He was making me become dependent upon Him for revelation. I had to become dependent upon Him to teach me the Scriptures.

The second verse He gave me was this: "In all your ways acknowledge Him, and He will direct your paths" (Prov. 3:6). I knew He was putting me on a new path and that I was going to start walking a different way as He directed me. Though I had quoted that verse hundreds of times before, He made it live to me during those months. A divine Person had moved into my spirit, and He began to reveal the Word of God to me. He took this professor and preacher who had taught this Book for years and said to me, in essence, "I am here now, and I am your teacher."

The Holy Spirit had to bring me to a place of willingness to admit I didn't know anything. I realized that I had not even understood that healing was a part of Jesus's atonement before I was healed. I had not believed that speaking in tongues was for us today until I received the baptism of the Holy Spirit at the time of my healing. So I had to admit I could be mistaken about other things I thought I knew. This was a place of dependence that I had not known before. The Holy Spirit would have to teach me how to walk this path.

The third verse He spoke to me was in Habakkuk: "For the vision is yet for an appointed time; but it speaks of the end, and does not lie. If it delays, wait for it; it will surely come, it will not delay" (Hab. 2:3). The verse preceding this one carries the instructions to write the vision and make it plain. In these many years following the direction the Holy Spirit gave me in seed form, it grew to become a mandate over my life. I did not know then that I would be privileged to share with the body of Christ the wonderful truths He revealed to me from His Word.

The fourth verse He quickened to my spirit during those months was this one: "If any of you lack wisdom, let him ask of God, who gives to all men liberally, and without criticism, and it will be given to him" (James 1:5). When I would read the Word or pray, these were the only Scriptures that lived to me. With time I came to a new place of surrender to the admonitions given in those four verses of Scripture.

Meanwhile, a "glory" cloud came to rest over my kitchen the day after I was healed. It was as if a literal cloud of His presence had moved in. It never left me. From the morning in April when I was healed until the night that divine revelation of the Word broke upon my mind, that cloud went everywhere I went. It got fuller and blacker, more "pregnant," like a cloudburst preparing to break. Although it was not visible to others, people who walked into my house could feel it. A Pentecostal pastor came to see me and asked, "Have you just been praying?" I replied, "No, I was just making biscuits." He said, "This place is full of God's presence." My husband responded, "It has been that way ever since my wife was healed."

When I went to the grocery store, that divine cloud of His presence hovered over my cart. It was over my automobile when I drove, and I could sense it over the foot of my bed at night. I was a Methodist professor who knew nothing about the spiritual world that I began experiencing after receiving the baptism of the Holy Spirit. Finally the day came when that glory cloud burst, and I was lost in the presence of God that broke in upon my mind and heart for twenty-two hours.

I had been invited to preach for the first time in a Pentecostal church. So overwhelming was the presence of God when that cloud burst, that the lady in whose home I was staying had to assist me in dressing for the meeting. When I stood up to preach, I couldn't speak. I just stood there and cried, experiencing the wonder of God's presence. The people came forward spontaneously to pray at the altar, and revival came to that church. For three months I ministered daily, simply sharing the fresh revelation that God had given me each day. The Book began to open to my understanding in revelation because I had met my teacher.

The greatest day of my life was the day I said, "I don't think I know anything." With that acknowledgment comes a brokenness of spirit that opens our minds to receive the wisdom He gives that is not of this world. Through my miraculous healing and baptism of the Holy Spirit, I was forced into a world where much of the theology I had taught for seventeen years didn't work anymore. I had to find out where I was. To get acquainted with the Holy Spirit, this wonderful third Person of the Godhead whom I had just met in a new dimension, I had to get into the Book.

So I got a lexicon, concordance, and notebook and categorized every verse in the Scriptures where I saw the Holy Spirit working (this was before today's computer software). I spent many hours a day for the next five years searching the Scriptures regarding this divine teacher. It was during those hours of study that I found He came to do sixty-six different works inside me. I learned that He had seven different moods and seven offices that He fulfilled.[2] Because of the dependence God worked in my life during those years, I gained insight into some beautiful truths that changed my life.

Jesus Himself said, "I can do nothing of Myself" (John 5:30). He taught His disciples the principle of abiding in Him in order to become fruitful. Without learning to abide in Christ, in dependence upon the Holy Spirit, all we will have is theory, up-and-down emotions, and a seeking for spiritual gifts. That is not what God intended as the Spirit-filled life. If we don't cooperate with the Holy Spirit, He can't do what the Father sent Him to do. So our total dependence on the Holy Spirit makes available to us the help we need from God. He doesn't expect us to be perfect; He came because we weren't perfect. He didn't come because we already knew, but because we don't know. He came to bring us what we don't have and can't receive in any other way.

Obedience

If our disposition must be one of dependence in order to walk in the Spirit, our response must be that of obedience to His Word. The first step of obedience is to hearken to what He says. We must be sure we are listening to His Word and set ourselves to hear Him. Often Jesus said, "He who has an ear, let him hear what the Spirit says" (Rev. 2:7). He told His disciples, "But blessed are...your ears, for they hear" (Matt. 13:16). Then after hearing Him, we must come to Him with a surrendered will so we can obey Him. The psalmist understood this when he declared, "The meek will He guide in judgment, and the meek He will teach His way" (Ps. 25:9). He has promised to guide the meek, those who are teachable. Those who are arrogant are not qualified to learn. No matter how much education we have, until we see our need of Him and cry out at the feet of Jesus, "I need the teacher," He cannot reveal His will to us. If we don't obey the Word we have received, why should we expect to receive more revelation? Sometimes we pray for more light when we haven't walked in the light we have received.

Peter declared that God has given the Holy Spirit to those who obey Him (Acts 5:32). Those who obey God will receive the baptism of the Holy Spirit. Many people have received this experience without understanding, doctrinally, what happened to them. They do not really know who this One is. They simply obeyed God, and He filled them with His Spirit. In that same way our continued obedience keeps our relationships growing and allows Him to continue to work in our lives.

Failure to continually walk in obedience will result in discontent and despondency. The cause of every despondent cloud that falls over the soul can be traced to the neglect of some particular instruction from our "divine monitor." Of course, this does not apply to places of testing where God may allow us to experience darkness for a season. It does explain, however, the difficult places we find ourselves in because we didn't listen to or obey the voice of the Spirit, but insisted that God let us go our own way.

Keeping in step

Not only must we learn obedience to walk in the Spirit, but we must also learn to *keep in step with Him* in our obedience. Oftentimes we fall way behind in our obedience, not finding a willingness in our hearts to commit to Him completely or depend on Him fully. A halfhearted obedience will not allow us to keep in step with His purposes in our lives.

Jesus called Himself the Good Shepherd and said that the sheep hear His voice (John 10:3, 11). Did you know that a shepherd does not keep all the sheep close to Him? A professional shepherd from Cyprus told me that sheep that walk close to the shepherd are those that choose to be there. As the shepherd stands among the sheep in the morning, he doesn't line them up in a certain order. He simply calls to them and begins to walk. When he calls, some of the sheep begin to run toward him, pushing others out of the way, to get to him first. These are the sheep that want to be close to the shepherd, to feel his touch and hear his voice. Others that want to kick around and do their own thing stay aloof from him.

The shepherd knows all the names of his sheep, but he can't talk to those that are not walking close to him. The ones he talks to the most as they walk along are those that keep in step with him, rubbing his leg to get his attention. What a picture of our Good Shepherd! He has given us the Holy Spirit to be our gentle guide—kind, tender, merciful, understanding. He is patient with us and willing to walk with us all the way. We need to acknowledge that we want to be near Him. Then we will do what is necessary to keep in step with our Lord.

Availability

As we learn to walk in step with our Lord, we will make ourselves available to Him to fulfill His purposes, not our own. Our continual *availability* is one of the greatest prerequisites for walking in the Spirit. The secret of abiding in Him is to continually make ourselves available as servants who are waiting for His instructions. This does not mean, however, that we have to try to "find" the will of God every day, begging Him for His presence and guidance.

It disturbs me to discover that some people are always trying to find the will of God. I don't believe I have to find what the will of God is for me every day. That doesn't mean I don't yield to the will of God continually, but I don't have to hear a word from God to tell me to do my ministry today. He gives guidance as it is needed, and He is faithful to show us when He needs to change our paths. Jesus promised He would be with us to the end. We must believe that He does not lie or leave us at every whim. Our responsibility is simply to rest in faith and to be available to His will.

Friendship

In order to walk in the Spirit, we also need to acknowledge that the Holy Spirit is our indwelling friend. Jesus called His disciples friends, and He told them it was expedient for Him to go away so He could send them the Comforter who would dwell in them. The Holy Spirit is our friend. How great a value we place on friendship will help determine how we value our relationship with the Holy Spirit.

A real friend is one who cuts covenant with you, promising not to leave you when you are facing trouble. One of my favorite definitions of a friend is "one who sees you through and through and understands the things you do, and keeps on pulling just for you."[3] When we walk in the Spirit, we are never without a friend. Never! When we feel lonely, it may be because we are looking only to people for friendship without reckoning that the One who dwells in us comes to bring us divine fellowship with the Godhead.

The Holy Spirit is not here to pet our sins or condone ungodliness; He will convict us when necessary. But He will also be with us in every time of need. We can count on Him in the painful situations of life. He is all-sufficient in every crisis, and He is our constant companion. He is the One who has undertaken our cause, and He expects us to call on Him when we need to know what to do in any situation. He wants to be included in the details of our lives. We might be surprised at what this friend would do for us if we asked for His help more often.

Fulfilling these prerequisites for walking in the Spirit will cause us to fulfill our destiny as believers and as the church. He is redeeming us back to relationship with God as He originally intended it should be. The first Adam chose to be independent from God; the last Adam lived in complete dependence upon

Him. As we choose to obey the Word of God and make ourselves available to be servants of God, walking closely to Him, we will find ourselves cultivating a divine friendship with Him. Cultivating this walk in the Spirit will result in eternal blessings for us and for His church.

RESULTS OF WALKING IN THE SPIRIT

God doesn't tell us to do something without a good reason. Everything He commands us to do is for our ultimate good. He doesn't make rules to be hard on us. They are to deliver us from destruction, to make life easier for us, and to allow us to live a life that is victorious over sin. He gave the Ten Commandments as an expression of His loving nature, to teach us how to relate to Him and to our fellow man.

When I was a young girl, I didn't understand that the reason my daddy made me come home at 10:30 p.m. was because he loved me and wanted to protect me; I thought he was being hard. Now I understand that his discipline and guidelines were proof that he cared for me. In that same way God proves His love to us by giving us His instructions for life that will make it possible to live in such a way that we can receive His blessings.

Deliverance from sin

One of the first blessings that comes as a result of walking in the Spirit is a complete and delightful deliverance from sin. Paul wrote, "But now, having been freed from sin and having become slaves of God, you have fruit unto holiness, and the end is eternal life" (Rom. 6:22). He taught that as we become servants of God, we will live holy lives and be freed from sin. He was declaring our freedom from the law of sin and death

(Rom. 7:6). In this same epistle Paul says clearly that if we live according to the flesh we will die, but if we yield to the Holy Spirit, we will know a life freed from the destructive power of sin. Daily walking in the Spirit is our only guarantee of having power over sin.

Peace

The second blessing of walking in the Spirit is that we will experience a delightful serenity, tranquility, and steadfastness. God's wonderful intention for His people is that they walk in peace, free from the tyranny of fleshly drives and impulses. There is a rest promised for the people of God that we will not find until we learn to live in the Spirit. As the Scriptures declare, "Therefore a rest remains for the people of God" (Heb. 4:9). Another simple way of describing that rest is to say that "we are at home in God."

In my home there is serenity, contentment, and peace. For me there is no place as peaceful as home. When I am away from home I am a "visitor." No matter how gracious the treatment I receive, it does not give me the sense of serenity and haven that my home does. Similarly the rest we find when we walk in the Spirit will be a haven to us. We will experience the peace of God and not be subject to ups and downs, becoming a victim of circumstances or of our own emotions. His rest gives us a stability in the face of every life situation.

God's providences

The third blessing that comes as a result of walking in the Spirit is the ability to meet the providences of God as they come to us with victory in our hearts. A "providence" is something that God chooses for us and promotes, although we may not always perceive it as something positive. We will be able to maintain perfect harmony between our inward disposition and His outward leadings or providences when we are walking in the Spirit.

Though we may be led through a difficult situation, our inside responses will be in harmony with it; we will not be disturbed. Of course, God doesn't bring to us the difficulties that are a result of sin. God doesn't promote divorce or other sinful behavior, for example (though we must remember that God loves the sinner and forgives). However, there are difficulties in our lives that God in His providence has permitted to cross our pathways for our ultimate good. Living in such a way that the providences of God can come into our lives always results in blessing.

For example, Simeon, the priest in the temple to whom Jesus was presented, probably didn't think his job was very significant—just keeping oil in the lamps. He could have become discouraged and said, "The glory is gone." By being faithful, however, he was in the right place at the right time to receive a blessing. When Mary brought her baby to the temple to be blessed, Simeon received the promise he had asked of God to see the salvation of the Lord. In the providence of God he lived to see the Messiah, and he recognized Him because of his walk with God (Luke 2:25–35). It was no accident that Jesus met the woman at the well. He was obeying His Father when He said He must "go through Samaria" (John 4:4). How many souls were saved that day because He obeyed the providence of God? We must learn to trust our unseen guide, sometimes without understanding or seeing results, but knowing we are obeying Him. When Philip, the evangelist, obeyed the instructions of the Holy Spirit to go to a desert, he met the Ethiopian eunuch who needed to know how to get saved (Acts 8). Because of Philip's obedience, a whole nation received the gospel in the providence of God. The Scriptures give many other examples as well of people who walked in obedience and received the providences of God.

If we don't walk in the Spirit, we too will miss the providences of God for the important decisions of life. I don't agree with those who say that we can marry anyone we want to and that God doesn't care about that decision. I think God should give direction concerning something as important as marriage. How can we trust God to work it out the rest of our lives if we don't trust Him to arrange it from the beginning? God's divine providences are just as needed in many other areas of guidance as well.

There will be many who receive rewards for having walked faithfully in the providences of God who never received recognition while on the earth. When God hands out rewards, it won't be just great preachers who are in the front of the line to receive them. Some of those little grandmothers who were locked up in the closet praying for the nations will be there as well. We may be surprised to see a Sunday school teacher who taught a junior boys' class faithfully for twenty years every Sunday as if it were the greatest congregation on earth, in the front of that line. Unless we learn to walk in the Spirit, we will miss some rich experiences that the providence of God would bring to our lives.

Walking in the Spirit brings great blessings to every life that surrenders to Him. First, as we have seen, it secures us in complete and delightful deliverance from sin (Gal. 5:16). Second, it enables us to have a serenity, tranquility, and steadfastness in our lives. And third, it enables us to meet the providences of God that He has ordained for us. Surely the requirements for walking in the Spirit are well worth the life of blessing and happiness God has ordained for His people.

We must remember that what God requires of us is always for our ultimate good. Then we will surrender our lives without reservation, becoming available to Him, dependent on Him, and learning to be obedient to His instructions. The greatest blessing of our learning to walk in the Spirit will be our deepening friendship with God. In learning to know the Holy Spirit, that blessed third Person of the Godhead, we will come into intimate relationship with God that will satisfy our hearts and fulfill the eternal purpose of God in us.

Appendix A

The Deity of the Holy Spirit as Affirmed by the Scriptures

1. He is spoken of as God.

> Why has Satan filled your heart to deceive the Holy Spirit...? You did not lie to men, but to God.
>
> —ACTS 5:3–4

> Do you not know that you are the temple of God, and that the Spirit of God dwells in you?
>
> —1 CORINTHIANS 3:16

> If anyone defiles the temple of God, God will destroy him. For the temple of God is holy. And you are His temple.
>
> —1 CORINTHIANS 3:17

> There are various gifts, but the same Spirit...the same Lord....It is the same God who operates all of them in all people.
>
> —1 CORINTHIANS 12:4–6

2. Divine names and titles are ascribed to Him.

The following names and titles used of the Holy Spirit prove His deity and oneness with the Father and the Son, and each one also unfolds another aspect of His divine personality.

> He is called Holy Ghost eighty-nine times in the King James Version.

> He is called Holy Spirit one hundred one times in the Modern English Version.

The Spirit of God (Gen. 1:2; 1 Sam. 19:20, 23; Matt. 3:16; 1 Cor. 3:1, 16, New English Bible)

The Spirit of the Living God (2 Cor. 3:3)

The Spirit of the Lord (Judg. 3:10; Isa. 11:2; 61:1; Luke 4:16–21)

The Spirit of Christ (Rom. 8:9; 1 Pet. 1:11)

The Spirit of His Son (Gal. 4:6)

The Spirit of Jesus Christ (Acts 16:7, New English Bible; Phil. 1:19)

The Spirit of Burning (Isa. 4:4)

The Spirit of Holiness (Rom. 1:4)

The Spirit of Promise (Acts 2:33; Eph. 1:13)

The Spirit of Truth (John 14:17; 15:26; 16:13; 1 John 4:6)

The Spirit of Life (Rom. 8:2; Rev. 11:11)

The Spirit of Wisdom (Isa. 11:1–2; Eph. 1:17)

The Spirit of Understanding (Isa. 11:1–2)

The Spirit of Counsel (Isa. 11:1–2)

The Spirit of Might (Isa. 11:1–2)

The Spirit of Knowledge (Isa. 11:1–2)

The Spirit of the Fear of the Lord (Isa. 11:1–2)

The Spirit of Grace (Zech. 12:10; Heb. 10:29)

The Spirit of Supplication (Zech. 12:10)

The Spirit of Glory and of God (1 Pet. 4:14)

The Spirit of Your Father (Matt. 10:20)

The Spirit of Prophecy (Rev. 19:10)

The Spirit of Adoption (Rom. 8:15)

The Spirit of Intercession (The Intercessor) (Rom. 8:26–29)

The Spirit of Judgment (Isa. 4:4; 28:6)

The Eternal Spirit (Heb. 9:14)

The Comforter (John 14:26; 15:26)

The Counselor (John 16:7)

The Teacher (Isa. 11:1–2; 61:1–2; John 14:16–17, 26; 15:25–26; 16:7–15; 1 Cor. 2:10–12)

My Spirit (Gen. 6:3)

Life (Greek, *neuma*, "breath," Rev. 13:15)

The Spirituals (1 Cor. 14:12)

The Glory (2 Cor. 3:8–18; 1 Pet. 4:14)

The Seven Horns (Rev. 5:6).

The Seven Eyes "Before the Throne" (Rev. 1:4–6; 3:1; 4:5; 5:6).

3. Divine attributes are ascribed to the Holy Spirit.

Eternity and self-existence (Heb. 9:14)

Omnipresence (Ps. 139:7–10)

Omnipotence (Luke 1:35; Acts 10:38)

Omniscience (John 14:26; 16:12–13; 1 Cor. 2:10–11)

Creation (Ps. 104:30; John 3:4–8)

Holiness (Rom. 1:4)

Love (Gal. 5:22–23)

Joy (Gal. 5:22–23)

Peace (Gal. 5:22–23)

Long-suffering (Gal. 5:22–23)

Gentleness (Gal. 5:22–23)

Goodness (Gal. 5:22–23)

Faith (Gal. 5:22–23)

Meekness (Gal. 5:22–23)

Self-control (Gal. 5:22–23)

Fellowship (Phil. 2:1)

Glory (2 Cor. 3:8–18; 1 Pet. 4:14)

Life (Rom. 8:10–13)

Wisdom (Isa. 11:2; 1 Cor. 12:8)

Knowledge (Isa. 11:2; 1 Cor. 12:8)

Immutability (Heb. 6:17)

Invisibility (John 3:8)

Appendix B

Scriptural Purposes
for the Gifts of Healing

1. To destroy the works of the devil (1 John 3:8).

2. To establish Jesus's astonishing claims (John 10:36–38).

3. To authorize the gospel message as preached by God's servants (Acts 4:29–30).

4. To establish the resurrection of Jesus (Acts 3:15–16).

5. To draw people to hear the good news of the gospel (John 6:2).

6. To turn people to God (Acts 9:34–35).

7. To convince the unbeliever of the truth of God's Word, mysterious though it may be (John 10:38).

8. To bring glory to God (Mark 2:12; Luke 13:17).

9. To inspire faith in God (John 2:23).

Notes

1—When He Is Come
Divine Mission

1. Author unknown.
2. George Smeaton, *The Doctrine of the Holy Spirit* (London: Banner of Truth Trust, 1958), 178.
3. Ibid.
4. G. Campbell Morgan, *The Gospel According to John* (New York: Fleming H. Revell Co., 1943).
5. Abraham Kuyper, *The Work of the Holy Spirit* (Grand Rapids, MI: Wm. Eerdmans Publication Co.).
6. Myer Pearlman, *Knowing the Doctrine of the Bible* (Springfield, MO: Gospel Publishing House, 1937), 306–307, emphasis added.

2—The Baptism of the Holy Spirit
Divine Enduement With Power

1. Scripture references to the order of receiving baptisms: Luke 3:16; Acts 1:8; 10:44–46; 11:15–16.
2. Scripture references to the baptism of repentance: Matt. 21:25; Mark 1:4; 11:30; Luke 3:3; 7:29; 20:4; Acts 1:22; 10:37; 13:24; 18:25; 19:3–4.
3. Scripture references to the baptism in water: Matt. 3:11, Mark 1:8; Luke 3:16; John 1:26, 28, 31, 33; Acts 1:5; 1 Pet. 3:21.
4. Scripture references to the baptism of the Holy Spirit: Matt. 3:11; Luke 3:16; Acts 11:16.

3—Gifts of the Holy Spirit
Part I: Divine Enablement to Know

1. Dr. Fuchsia Pickett, *The Holy Spirit Manual*, from the Outline Study Series, 14.

4—Gifts of the Holy Spirit
Part II: Divine Enablement to Do

1. Author unknown.
2. Source unknown.

3. The study of these gifts was compiled from notes written by Dr. Judson Cornwall for home fellowship group studies when he was associate pastor at Fountaingate Ministries in Dallas, Texas.

6—The Fruit of the Spirit
Part I: Divine Character Defined

1. Perry Brewster, *Pentecostal Doctrine* (Cheltenham, England: Reed Hearst Publishers, 1976).

2. Samuel Chadwick, *The Way to Pentecost* (New York: Fleming H. Revell Co., 1937).

3. D. L. Moody, *Notes From My Bible, From Genesis to Revelation* (New York: Fleming H. Revell Co., 1895).

7—The Fruit of the Spirit
Part II: Divine Love, Joy, Peace, Long-Suffering, and Gentleness

1. Fuchsia Pickett, *God's Dream* (Shippensburg, PA: Destiny Image Publishers, 1991). This 140-page book deals with this theme completely.

2. Melody Green is director of Last Day Ministries in Lindale, Texas.

8—The Fruit of the Spirit
Part III: Divine Goodness, Faith, Meekness, and Temperance

1. Brewster, *Pentecostal Doctrine*.

2. Martin Luther, *Commentary on Galatians*, trans. by Theodore Graebner (Grand Rapids, MI: Zondervan Pub. House, 1939).

3. William Edward Vine, *Expository Dictionary of the New Testament Words* (Old Tappan, NJ: Fleming H. Revell Co., 1966).

4. Chadwick, *The Way to Pentecost*.

10—Walking in the Spirit
Part II: Divine Requirements
and Blessings

1. Andrew Murray, *Humility* (Springdale, PA: Whitaker House, 1982), 10.

2. Fuchsia Pickett, *Presenting the Holy Spirit: Who Is He? Vol. 1,* (Shippensburg, PA: Destiny Image Publishers, 1993).

3. Author unknown.

EMPOWERED
TO RADICALLY CHANGE
YOUR WORLD

Charisma House brings you books, e-books, and other media from dynamic Spirit-filled Christians who are passionate about God.

Check out all of our releases from best-selling authors like **Jentezen Franklin**, **Perry Stone**, and **Kimberly Daniels** and experience God's supernatural power at work.